A PSYCHOLOGIST DE[SCRIBES] HER EXPERIENCE WORKING IN THE DANGEROUS AND UNPREDICTABLE WORLD OF THE FEDERAL PRISON SYSTEM

By focusing on her experience working in the Federal Bureau of Prisons, a female psychologist gives an account of the world inside the system. Prisons are highly structured environments with specific policies and procedures to ensure consistent orderliness, yet simultaneously there exists an ever-present underlying turbulence that threatens to erupt at any time. At higher security prisons these eruptions occur all too often, and can range from absurd behaviors, like self-administered liposuction, to serious assaults and gruesome murders. *As I Live and Breathe* provides a glimpse into the federal prison system and highlights some of the challenges correctional workers face when tasked with managing extreme criminals in a dangerous and unpredictable world.

I didn't always believe in the existence of these convoluted examples of our species; these individuals with "as if personalities," acting as if they are human. There was a time when I believed criminal behavior was primarily due to circumstances. I believed many of these people had a poor upbringing, had developed a drug addiction due to biochemical unluckiness, had made a series of bad decisions, or were the victims of social injustices. I also believed all inmates would benefit from the opportunity for self-improvement. If treated with respect, anyone could become a productive member of society, even if their society was limited to the world inside the walls of a prison.

Many people have this same perspective—the fundamental belief that people are good or, at a minimum, can become good, given the right set of circumstances. Managing maximum-security inmates—those that are generally described as the "worst of the worst"—changed my view. These inmates don't respond to basic correctional interventions; yet, they still have to be managed by correctional staff.

"...a heartfelt, dynamic testimonial to a great career in a difficult field...personal, insightful...gives a clear illustration of the dangers of working inside a prison..."—*1st Lt. Gary F. Cornelius, Deputy Sheriff, Retired, Fairfax County (VA), Adjunct Faculty: George Mason University.*

"...During my tenure as Warden at USP Marion I quickly learned to trust advice and insight from Dr. Patterson...Dr. Patterson has captured the essence of how corrections changes staff..."—*J. Walton, Warden, Marion, Retired.*

"...realistic picture of life inside Federal prison facilities...an honest description of a bizarre culture, comprised of psychopaths, pedophiles, and other sex offenders, substance abusers, and those suffering from an array of mental health and personality disorders... —*Dr. Paul M. Lucko, Chair, Department of Community Leadership and Human Services, Murray State University*

ATHE

_ _ , . ..ᴜᴜ. � sychologist

Marla Patterson

Moonshine Cove Publishing, LLC

Abbeville, South Carolina U.S.A.
FIRST MOONSHINE COVE EDITION January 2019

ISBN: 978-1-945181-51-1
Library of Congress PCN: 2019868232

Cover Images public domain, cover design by Moonshine Cove Staff

About the Author

Marla Patterson, Ph.D. retired from the Federal Bureau of Prisons in 2014 after working at the agency for nearly 24 years. She started working for the prison system as an intern at the Federal Correctional Institution (FCI) in Ft. Worth, Texas, worked seven years as a drug treatment specialist at FCI Seagoville, Texas, and in 1999 started working at the United States Penitentiary (USP) Leavenworth. In 2002, she transferred to USP Marion where she was promoted to Chief Psychologist in 2004. Dr. Patterson received a master's degree from Bradley University and a doctoral degree from the University of North Texas. Since retiring, she teaches part-time, travels and enjoys time with her family.

marlakpatterson.com

Dedication

In memory of Elizabeth Fields, a remarkable person.

Acknowledgment

I would like to express my gratitude to those who assisted, knowingly and unknowingly, with the completion of this book. To my amazingly patient husband, Mercer, who read, reread, discussed, advised and then read again.

To Mariah Patterson for your support and help with developing ideas, Lori Sistrunk who helped with editing, and Lynn Gray who gave great feedback.

To Mickey McGee and Jackson Fredman for your suggestions.

To Gary F. Cornelius who went way beyond my expectation in providing encouragement and assistance.

To Gene D. Robinson at Moonshine Cove Publishing for your willingness to tolerate me and all my questions.

Most importantly, to all the dedicated correctional workers. Thank-you for helping to keep society safe.

As I Live
and
Breathe

USP Leavenworth

USP Marion

Preface

I've come to believe there are people among us that simply aren't human. They're unaffected by the emotions and motivations that are part of the normal human experience. These beings stab their children, stash them under their beds, and continue living in their home until the stench brings attention to their residence. They rape their three-year-old granddaughter and yet feel themselves justified when chronically yelling profane and degrading remarks at correctional officers. They call their elderly mother from prison and demand she talk dirty to them — a request that clearly causes distress to the mother. They impersonate a physician, gain access to communities of vulnerable refugees, and then target adolescents whom they later rape and kill. They stab another inmate so viciously and vigorously they have to stop and rest in the middle of the attack before continuing with their mission. Only when enough staff arrive on the scene do they lay down the weapon and submit to restraints.

It may be difficult for the average person to believe, but these individuals usually aren't intellectually limited or seriously mentally ill.

They often have a good sense of reality, organized thoughts, and an absence of delusions. They show no indication of experiencing hallucinations, excess energy or sleep/appetite disturbances. With the exception of the presence of a severe personality disorder, there's no diagnosis for what plagues them.

Their real problem is a fundamental incapacity to feel compassion, empathy, or genuine attachment — an inability to value others beyond the superficial use they can serve at any moment. There are theories as to cause and research to support the idea that their brains are wired differently. Regardless of the etiology, I know it exists in this extreme form. And, although those who've never actually worked with these individuals might disagree, there's currently no realistic treatment for their dysfunction. At this level, it's an unsolvable, unfixable problem. There's no healing them. They cannot be refurbished or rehabilitated. And what makes them most dangerous is they can disguise their depravity at will.

I didn't always believe in the existence of these convoluted examples of our species; these individuals with "as if personalities," acting as if they are human. There was a time when I believed criminal behavior was primarily due to circumstances. I believed many of these people had

a poor upbringing, had developed a drug addiction due to biochemical unluckiness, had made a series of bad decisions, or were the victims of social injustices.

I also believed all inmates would benefit from the opportunity for self-improvement. If treated with respect, anyone could become a productive member of society, even if their society was limited to the world inside the walls of a prison. Many people have this same perspective — the fundamental belief that people are good or, at a minimum, can become good, given the right set of circumstances.

Managing maximum-security inmates — those that are generally described as the "worst of the worst" — changed my view.

During my twenty-four-year career with the Bureau of Prisons, I worked exclusively with male inmates at four federal institutions and at every security level: minimum, low, medium, high, and maximum. The vast majority of inmates are managed with basic behavior-modification techniques: reward good behavior, punish bad behavior, be consistent. Most adapt and complete their sentences without issues. Some even benefit from it.

At higher level facilities, there are a subset of inmates who are not amenable to these basic correctional interventions; yet, they still have to be

managed by correctional staff. As difficult as it is working with these inmates, it's worse when there's a lack of understanding by society of what occurs inside this closed system. When conceptualizing the treatment of others, we tend to imagine how we'd respond if put in a similar situation. The fundamental fallacy here is the idea we're all the same and would respond the same. We aren't the same and we don't respond the same. The golden rule doesn't always work in high-security prisons.

The supervision of these inmates is enormously complicated and became increasingly more complicated during my tenure. The challenges were amplified by poor, policy-related decisions that were being made by those outside the system — those who were uninformed and misguided.

I know everyone is entitled to their opinion, but I believe I've actually earned mine, which brings me to the reason for this book.

I watched as procedures and national policy regarding the treatment of inmates changed. I listened to public opinion that ranged from the belief that inmates were abused and neglected to the belief they were overindulged and coddled. Many of these opinions were clearly made not based on direct experience but from information gleaned from books, articles, and testimonies provided by inmates. Well-intentioned individuals

listened to their incarcerated loved ones or visited facilities in a professional capacity, conducted interviews, and drew conclusions. It seemed much of the information being gathered was one-sided and lacking in accuracy. Even when concerns were valid, inadequate consideration was given to "solutions," which resulted in new difficulties.

It's quite clear there are many naïve, uninformed, and good-hearted individuals on the outside who are quick to commiserate with inmates. There's an overabundance of the benevolent in society who sympathize with inmates and/or impose policies that are unrealistic or detrimental to the correctional environment. It's my goal in writing this book to have you, the reader, consider the other side — some of the things you haven't been told. This book is an attempt to educate the public and, hopefully, decision-makers about some of the real challenges that face correctional staff.

The examples I give in this book are from my own experience. I've heard plenty of stories from long-time staff members that include even more horrendous and extreme examples than I give, but that's their story to tell. This is mine.

CHAPTER 1: The Muse

There are many days in my career I don't remember. There are days and experiences I want to remember, and there are moments I'll never forget. One of the latter was the day I decided to put my work experience into printed words.

I was across the street from the main institution of USP Marion, at the satellite prison camp (SCP), the minimum-security facility. Camps are usually located near high- and medium-security institutions to help with work that needs to be done outside the fence or wall but still on the grounds of the facility. Camp inmates provide these services, which include attending to the landscape, working in warehouses, and maintaining outside buildings such as the institution power plant and staff housing. The Marion SCP is located in a federal wildlife refuge that's bounded on one side by a forest. It's an unfenced institution that, at the time, housed around 250 male inmates.

These inmates usually had relatively short sentences (less than ten years) and were considered non-violent. Inmates at camps are on the honor system most of the day and are expected to remain on the prison grounds or at their job site.

Most are assigned jobs, many of them menial. They have the opportunity to access some recreational activities: a small weight shack, handball court, basketball court, running track, softball field, arts and crafts area, gardening facilities. They also have access to education classes, religious services, and psychology groups. In addition, there are some vocational training programs offered such as wastewater treatment. But, overall, there's not a lot to do. The majority of inmates at the camp follow the rules, at least enough to not get into serious trouble. Most inmates are geographically close to their families and have frequent visitors. This is a powerful motivator for inmates at this security level.

I used to go to the camp a few times per week to meet with incoming inmates as they went through a process called Admissions and Orientation, introducing them to the policies and expectations of the camp. All the inmates were also seen individually to assess medical and psychological needs. If need be, they'd be seen on a routine basis to ensure adequate care.

I was talking with an SCP inmate when I heard a call come over the radio. Something was going on in the penitentiary, in L Unit. I finished talking to the inmate, locked up the office, dropped off my keys at the control center, got into my car, and drove back to the main facility. The camp and

penitentiary weren't far from each other, but to get to the main entrance at the front of the building was a bit of a jaunt. I always drove as opposed to waiting for the institution van, which was driven by an inmate. About fifteen years prior, I'd been part of a well-written mock training scenario in which a van-driving inmate took a staff member hostage. I never forgot it and preferred to never again get into an inmate-driven van.

There was no huge hurry to get inside L unit, mostly because, even if I had been in a hurry, there was no way I could get there fast and there was plenty of staff to respond who were closer, quicker, and stronger. If I'd already been inside the facility, I'd certainly have been running to help out. As it was, I was back inside within fifteen minutes.

Entering the main facility always reminded me of Maxwell Smart entering CONTROL headquarters — all the electronic opening and closing of barriers by some unseen presence. I passed through four grilles — gates with a series of one-inch-diameter, vertical, high-grade steel bars — before getting to our control center, the place where I received my keys and radio. The first three grilles were interlocking, which meant each must close completely before the next could open. Although the fourth wasn't interlocking, it was never opened without the prior grille being closed. Thus, progression into the facility was always a bit

slow. I stopped at the control center to pick up keys and a radio. After passing through two more grilles and walking down the north corridor, I saw several officers coming toward me wheeling an inmate on a gurney.

We reached the Health Services door at about the same time. I planned to just keep going down the hall toward my office with a quick stop in L Unit to see if I could help with anything. The telephone on the wall rang, so I stopped to answer it. The officers and the man on the gurney were next to me. The control room officer on the other end of the phone wanted to know the name of the inmate on the gurney.

I looked at the inmate, who was unconscious. I didn't recognize him despite the fact I'd seen him at least once a week for two years. His left eye was hanging out of its socket. His face was swollen, beefy, and disfigured. His skin was blue-gray, a color of skin I'd never seen before. One of the officers said, "He looks dead." I considered the statement seriously and then thought, *Well, I guess he does.* It didn't dawn on me immediately, but that was exactly how he looked. It turned out the inmate was Russo. Another inmate had attacked him in L Unit. Russo had recently been released from the Special Housing Unit (SHU). I'd later learn he'd be in a coma for the rest of his life, a life that would end just a few years later.

Russo had transferred to USP Marion in December 2003 from one of the Bureau of Prison's medical centers, where he'd been sent from the Administrative Maximum Facility (ADX) Florence. The ADX couldn't manage him due to unending incidents of insolence, threatening behavior, throwing and smearing feces, destroying property, and assaulting staff. They had ultimately concluded he was mentally ill and referred him for an evaluation. The medical center deemed him not mentally ill, and the powers-that-be decided to transfer him to USP Marion. Generally, inmates are returned to their sending institution once evaluations or treatment has been completed at a medical facility. On rare occasions, they're re-designated due to security reasons or to give staff a break from particularly difficult inmates. Russo was a particularly difficult inmate.

Physically, he appeared primeval and could have been the Missing Link. His arms, legs, and torso were very strong despite his undefined, slovenly appearance. His head was strikingly similar to a Neanderthal, and his expression perpetually conveyed disdain. He could easily break hand restraints with forearms that rivaled Popeye's. Russo offended staff and inmates on an almost daily basis. He'd yell up and down the SHU range from his secured cell, heaving insults and threats

at dangerous inmates. And, of course, the inmates would yell back.

It isn't unusual for these types of interactions to occur between various inmates, but usually the taunting is launched by the more menacing inmate toward a weaker inmate for entertainment purposes. Staff respond by moving the inmates to different ranges. Russo, however, was able to offend inmates regardless of where he was placed.

He had the same presentation with staff, doling out insults and threats. His primary targets were the medical staff, who were required to bring him daily general medication (as opposed to psychiatric medication). He'd occasionally attempt to grab one of them; fortunately, he was unsuccessful. His main complaint was that he wanted Xanax, a highly addictive, anti-anxiety medication. He wouldn't tolerate being told no, so he spent most of his days yelling at staff and inmates from his cell and throwing feces.

Russo had recently been let out of the Special Housing Unit, where he'd been separated from other inmates at all times. He had spent almost all his time at Marion in SHU because he rarely followed rules. His release from the unit was a bureaucratic decision. Given that SHU was highly restrictive, there'd always been pressure from above to get inmates out of that unit as soon as possible. SHU was an area that was considered

particularly concerning and perhaps cruel by those who've never worked in a prison setting.

On the day of the assault, both Russo and the assailant came out of their respective cells at the same time for recreation. They exchanged words and Russo took a swing at the assailant, but missed. The assailant swung back and didn't miss. Russo fell to the ground and was kicked a few times. The assailant then used a homemade knife and commenced to stabbing Russo numerous times, stopping when Russo stopped moving and continuing whenever Russo twitched. Russo suffered punctures in his neck that severed his spinal cord, in his face and in his lungs; and one of his eyes was intentionally gorged out of the socket. The other inmates stood around watching with an apparently complete lack of interest, waiting to return to their cells.

Inmates are very creative when it comes to having weapons in prison. At higher-security facilities, these are usually shivs or homemade knives called "shanks." They're constructed out of any piece of metal or hard plastic and sharpened to a point by repeatedly rubbing the blade on metal or concrete. The handle is usually made of pieces of material wrapped tightly at one end of the device. Shanks are all too common in this environment. Staff constantly find and confiscate them, and

inmates constantly find new ways to make and hide them.

I saw the assailant the next day when I was making rounds in SHU. I remembered talking to him when he first came to Marion. He seemed like a kid then. Hell, he still seemed like a kid except for the fact he had just committed this atrocity. The inmate looked at me, shrugged his shoulders slightly, smirked, and said dispassionately, "Shit happens. I guess I had a bad day." He could have been talking about the weather. He didn't want to give details or discuss it. He also didn't want to answer questions regarding risk factors for suicide. At USP Marion, after-action reports on suicide had indicated a trend. Suicide attempts were frequently preceded by serious assaults. The inmate gave assurances he was fine and had no plans to engage in self-harm. This was all I could get out of him.

The staff's emotional reaction to the assault was cold and indifferent. So was mine. In the past, I hadn't been like that. I was aware of my growing callousness, and it was clear that most of the other staff weren't aware of theirs. It was at this point I was struck with a fleeting desire to someday write a book about working in corrections. I made a mental note to start logging my experiences.

CHAPTER 2: Government Roots

When I was young, my father, who was self-employed, often talked about those who had government jobs. I think he envied the idea of a guaranteed paycheck and good benefits regardless of performance level. I didn't pay a lot of attention to these things, as I'd already decided to become a psychologist. The decision to work in a helping profession was made when I was in eighth grade while watching *The Bob Newhart Show*. He seemed to have a good job and I liked the idea of working with people like Mr. Elliot Carlin, a character on the show who presented as an entertainingly neurotic and morose mental health patient.

Years later, I began a doctorate-level internship at a federal prison, the Federal Correctional Institution (FCI) in Ft. Worth, Texas (this institution has since become a Federal Medical Center). I chose this internship because it was close to where I was living, it paid well, and they accepted me.

I'd never been inside a prison prior to starting the internship, and I expected to see Tony Montana

and James Cagney characters everywhere. My experience was very different from my expectation. FCI Ft. Worth was a low-security facility with a large geriatric population. It had several separate buildings surrounding an expansive, well-tended yard. It looked like a college campus quad. When the weather was nice — which was often — the yard was populated by numerous old men in wheelchairs who would sit and talk as long as they were allowed.

In general, the inmates were pleasant. Other than being in prison, they were indistinguishable from individuals I'd worked with at an outpatient clinic. There was no violence.

My biggest concern was trying to not be crapped on by the birds that roosted in the trees. If the inmates made a loud sound or clapped while a staff member was walking underneath a tree, it would rain down. This was the extent of their misconduct during the year I was there.

The Bureau of Prisons does a good job recruiting interns, and I was no exception. As my internship was coming to an end, I heard that the FCI in Seagoville, Texas, near Dallas, was looking for Drug Treatment Specialists to start a new 500-hour residential drug program. Given my positive experience at Ft. Worth and reflecting on my father's words, I decided to pursue a career with the federal government. I was able to transfer

directly from one position to the other with no lag time. The pay was good enough, there was plenty of vacation and holiday leave, and I started contributing to my retirement account as soon as I could.

The down side to being so comfortable with my job was I lost the desire to complete my doctorate degree in psychology. I worked at Seagoville for more than seven years as a Drug Treatment Specialist, a position that required a master's or a bachelor's degree with experience. Despite nearly constant harassment from my supervisor and others (they would call it "encouragement"), I just wasn't interested in completing my doctoral dissertation, the only missing requirement to complete my Ph.D. Finally, after years of ignoring it, I muscled up the motivation and did what had to be done. I'd completed all the coursework for the doctorate within five years, but it took another seven years to get that dissertation done.

Within months of getting my Ph.D., a colleague of my husband's convinced him to apply for a lieutenant position at the United States Penitentiary (USP) in Leavenworth. Leavenworth was known to be a very tough, high-security institution, but it was considered a good career move, so we moved to Kansas.

Initially, I took another position as a Drug Treatment Specialist because there were no

psychologist positions open. That actually was my most enjoyable year working for the Bureau of Prisons (BOP). My office was at the satellite prison camp (SPC). The camp was adjacent to and northwest of the penitentiary, within walking distance if you were up for a bit of a stroll. I split my time between the minimum-security inmates at the SPC, who always claimed to be innocent, and the high-security inmates at the USP, who readily embraced their guilt. I primarily conducted drug education groups.

The balance and contrast were what I liked most about my job during that year. SPC inmates tended to complain about trivial matters, and that can be tiring after a while. The USP inmates tended to be misanthropic, which can also be tiring after a while. I was able to create my own programming schedule, starting the day at one facility, then getting into my car and driving past the buffalo pen on the corner to arrive at the other facility and finishing the day there. I enjoyed the versatility and the opportunity to work with the two extremes on the scale of criminality.

I was promoted to a supervisory psychologist position after one year. My office, and the offices of the four treatment specialists I supervised, were located in C-cell house. All inmates in that unit participated in a residential program that focused primarily on criminal thinking and cognitive

distortions. My role was pivotal to the future positions I'd hold in the USP system.

After several years at Leavenworth, my husband and I wanted to move on, move out, and get out. It's difficult to transfer together as a couple to a new institution and nearly impossible to do so to a desirable location. USP Marion, in Marion, Illinois, had positions available for both my husband and me, and neither of us would have to demote. In 2002, I took a position as a Drug Abuse Program Coordinator and my husband lateraled as a lieutenant. At that time, the psychology department at Marion consisted of a Chief Psychologist, a Drug Treatment Specialist, and me. From the day I got there, the Chief Psychologist introduced me as the heir apparent. And, sure enough, when he retired two years later, I was selected as the Chief Psychologist. Over time, the psychology department grew to a staff of eighteen, encompassing a residential drug abuse program and two sex-offender management programs. I held the position of Chief until I retired in December 2014.

CHAPTER 3: Comforts of Marion

As you can imagine, working at high-security prisons like those at Leavenworth and Marion is very different from working in low-security prisons. Staff members tend to be much more hardened, security is tighter, there's more violence, and there's a general increase in the level of ruthlessness among inmates. Despite that, inmates at higher-security level facilities are offered the same amount of programming and relatively the same opportunities for self-improvement as those at the lower-security facilities. Even though there are more correctional officers and more controlled movement at the higher-security institutions, the management over the facilities is similar.

When I started my career, USP Leavenworth was considered to be a level-five security institution on a six-point scale. There was only one level-six facility and that was USP Marion. The point system was eventually changed and institutions were ranked as minimum-, low-, medium-, high-, and maximum-security facilities. From 1994 to 2006, there were two institutions considered maximum security in the federal

system: USP Marion and Administrative Maximum Security (ADX) Florence, in Colorado. Currently, the only maximum-security facility, also called a supermax, is ADX Florence. However, another institution is expected to be activated to help with the most difficult inmates. In 2012, the Bureau of Prison purchased a dormant and ravaged State facility from Illinois. This enormous institution, which is in northern Illinois is expected to house a large population of maximum-security inmates.

I was a little nervous but also excited about working at USP Leavenworth. It was a huge facility with a wealth of historical significance. It was one of the original three institutions established by Congress to hold federal prisoners. The prison first housed inmates in 1903. It was built with a huge dome in the center and forty-foot-high walls. The curb appeal was impressive — immense and majestic. The inside was extraordinary but old and dank. Most of the living quarters had been renovated and thus a little less dingy. Overall, the facility had a lot of nooks and crannies, and isolated and distant places; that, along with the types of inmates it housed, made it a dangerous place to work.

When I worked there, there were five, very large open units and three smaller units. In addition, there was a new Special Housing Unit (SHU) for

inmates who failed to comply with the rules, and another secured unit for SHU overflow, known as D (Dog)-cell house.

Dog-cell house was something out of one of those old James Cagney movies. It was five stories high with two-man cells, traditional cell doors with steel bars, and a small catwalk that ran down the length of each tier. The cell house was known for housing many Mariel Boatlift Cubans who were transferred to Leavenworth after rioting at other facilities in 1987. The Mariel Boatlift was an emigration agreement from then-President Carter and Fidel Castro in the 1980s. The result was a mass emigration of Cubans. The majority of these 125,000 immigrants were law-abiding; however, Castro had also released Cubans from jails and mental health facilities to join the exodus. Many of the "Mariels" who arrived were granted immigration parole, meaning they were allowed to enter the country despite not meeting all the usual criteria to enter the country as an immigrant. It was a humanitarian act, a nice gesture, however, a problem arose when any of these individuals engaged in criminal activity. It was easy enough to appropriately sentence them to a term of imprisonment in the United States, but once their sentence was completed and their immigration parole was revoked, they couldn't be deported. Cuba sure didn't want them back, and no other

nation was willing to accept them. So they remained in prison.

By the late 1980s, there were around 2500 Cuban detainees held in federal prisons who'd completed their sentences. In 1987, the media began broadcasting plans by the United States to deport these 2500 detainees to Cuba (which was later rescinded). The detainees did not want to be returned to Cuba. Many believed they would be put to death by Castro. The news of the planned deportation set off 13 days of rioting at USP Atlanta and the Federal Detention Center in Oakdale, Louisiana. Dog-cell house at Leavenworth was made available to house the instigators of and participants in those riots. The Cubans remained locked down in the unit for several years. Eventually, they were transferred to other facilities or released.

When I worked at Leavenworth, Dog-cell house was the only unit that hadn't been recently renovated. The ceiling was high and there was nothing to absorb sound. It could definitely get loud in there. The insulation was poor, paint was peeling from every surface. Since the catwalks were narrow and immediately adjacent to the cells which had grilles (as opposed to steel doors), it was easy to throw nasty concoctions as staff walked by. Thus, the unit generally housed inmates who had engaged in misconduct but were not considered

high risk for assaulting staff. Despite that, staff were still occasionally assaulted in Dog cell house. And I was one of them. The unit was later condemned and remained vacant for years.

For a brief period, there was another building, known as building 63, that was also used as a Special Housing Unit. This was a building of particular character; it was where Robert Stroud, the *Birdman of Alcatraz,* actually did his bird research and became "The Birdman." It may not be well known, but Stroud was inaccurately portrayed in the 1962 movie starring Burt Lancaster. He wasn't mild-mannered. Besides his three murders — one of which was that of a correctional officer — he was a predatory homosexual and considered to be vicious by both staff and fellow inmates.

Building 63 was a really old, dungeon-like structure. It had been out of commission for a long period of time before the warden reopened it in 2001. I believe this decision had something to do with the closing of Lorton Reformatory, which was operated by the District of Columbia Department of Corrections. All of the inmates at that facility were to be absorbed by the Bureau of Prisons, and USP Leavenworth certainly got its fair share. As anticipated, many of these inmates had difficulty adjusting to the federal system and ended up in the Special Housing Unit.

The cells and corridors of Building 63 were dark and the walls were constructed of brick. There was no air conditioning and poor ventilation. The plumbing was inadequate. Some of the cells were tucked away down alcoves that were so dark you could barely see inside the cells. To say the building was dilapidated would be an understatement. Eventually, the demand for additional SHU space diminished and the building was closed. It was later condemned, although I felt like it met that criteria long before it officially happened.

The new Special Housing Unit at Leavenworth was a modern building with a control center located in the middle of four hallways. Three of the hallways had two stories, each lined with cells on both sides. The cell accommodations were for two men and included a shower in the cell and a secured window for outside lighting. The doors were controlled electronically, and cameras were used for additional monitoring of inmate movement. There were inside and outside recreation cages. This SHU was always full. Most interactions between staff and inmates occurred at the recreation cages or while standing in front of the solid-metal cell doors. There was a small speaker in the door to assist with this interaction.

When I transferred from Leavenworth to Marion, I went from working in an open-population institution of around 1700 inmates to working in a

locked-down institution of 400 inmates, with all amenities under one roof. The difference was startling. At Leavenworth, there were 400 inmates in the Special Housing Unit alone.

Marion felt like a breath of fresh air. It was more secure and smaller than any facility where I'd worked. There was no contact with any untethered inmate. This means, if there was no iron grille — a protective barrier of metal bars — between you and the inmate, the inmate was in handcuffs and leg irons.

At Marion, there were no inmates in the hallways unless you ran into one who was in restraints. Inmates moving around the institution were always escorted by at least two correctional officers who had their hands on the inmate to maintain physical control at all times.

Some staff members — perhaps in an effort to impress — told me there were assaults every week at Marion. This simply wasn't true. Compared to Leavenworth, there were rarely fights, and, when one did occur, the fight was always contained by a grille or fence. Staff would stand and wait for enough support to arrive before entering a unit or a range on a unit. Ranges are separated tiers or divisions within a unit. This was so different from Leavenworth, where assaults happened much more frequently and staff didn't have the luxury of waiting for support. Action had to be taken

immediately. There were no physical barriers between staff and the inmates in the general population at Leavenworth.

I think I smiled for the first month I was at Marion. The halls were quiet as opposed to walking down the hall or up stairwells at Leavenworth where it was me, maybe a few other staff members, and a hundred inmates all around moving to their destinations. At Marion, the units were much smaller and everything was contained. Officers were much more cognizant of other staff members.

As I grew familiar with USP Marion and came to know the inmates, my comfort level slowly changed. It's true, they didn't fight as often, but when they did, it was barbaric. Some were very creative in their weaponry, making spears so they could assault staff from a distance as opposed to using a garden-variety shiv. Over a short period, my primary goals of helping inmates with criminal thinking problems, substance abuse and mental health issues quickly morphed into the goals of tamping down severe personality disorders, helping staff manage and cope, and protecting the BOP from frivolous lawsuits. Preventing suicide and self-harm was always important.

In 2002, USP Marion and the ADX in Florence were considered to be the only maximum-custody federal institutions in the Bureau of Prisons system. Ideally, inmates who needed to be

separated from one another would never be in the same facility. However, since there were only two maximum-custody facilities, this wasn't possible. As a result, USP Marion and ADX Florence housed separatees (inmates from whom other inmates needed to be separated for reasons of safety or collusion) within the same institution but on different ranges or units. These were the only two facilities in which this was allowed. This could be accomplished because of the design of the facilities and the procedures in place to keep inmates on units separate from one another.

Placement of inmates was a huge chess game. Many inmates, as well as their suspected associates, had to be kept separate from certain other inmates within the facility. At other institutions, inmates could easily change units because it was a foregone conclusion there was no one in the facility that required separation. Inmates are separatees for a variety of reasons and can be given this status at any time — during pretrial or during incarceration. If two or more inmates require separation at mainline (regular) institutions, the information is placed in their permanent record and at least one of them is transferred to another facility. This is to ensure the inmate is safe from any known threat. Therefore, when inmates want to change cells, cellmates, jobs,

etc., the decision can be made easily by the unit team members in charge of housing assignments.

However, at Marion, every move from one unit to another or one range to another had to be reviewed by a special committee. Inmates who had prior assaults or fights with other inmates clearly couldn't be housed on the same range and usually not even in the same unit. However, there was a plethora of soft signs that led staff to suspect other problems even if the inmates hadn't actually come to blows. In these cases, staff attempted to keep inmates apart without having enough information to make it official. Predetermining which inmates would have issues with one another was nearly impossible, and yet a mistake could result in a serious assault or worse. The committee — which, at a minimum, consisted of an associate warden, captain, investigative lieutenant, unit managers, case manager coordinator, and a psychologist — would meet weekly and discuss any information they had regarding the inmate in question before any move was made.

When I transferred to Marion in 2002, the facility consisted of eight units: one Special Housing Unit, six "general population" units, and a transition unit. The institution was laid out in a basic cross shape, with all the units on two long hallways. Down one hallway were the doors to five

units and down the other were the doors to three units, one of which was SHU.

The general population units were each divided into either two or four small ranges, with several layers of security. After entering the cell house through a locked steel door that was opened with a Folger-Adams key (the standard, large brass prison key), which was held by the unit officer, there was a small landing. On one side were concrete steps leading up to the second floor and on the other were concrete steps leading down to the lower ranges. Basically, there were two two-story ranges, that were back to back in some units, or two two-story ranges that faced each other in other units. Unlike most prisons recently built, in which an officer can pretty much see all ranges from a central location, in these cell houses, an officer could see only one range at a time. The units held 72 inmates, 18 inmates on each range.

Cells were as you would imagine. They were small, six feet by eight feet, with a concrete slab that served as a bed platform; a mattress with built-in pillow; a stainless-steel, toilet-and-sink combination; a concrete shelf for toiletries; a concrete or steel shelf/desk; and a reflective plaque mounted to the concrete wall to be used as a mirror.

When I arrived at Marion, all units and most of the institution (with the exception of staff offices) weren't air-conditioned. [There were four new units

built in 2004 that were air conditioned, and eventually the food service area was air conditioned.] In the summer, Marion is very hot and extremely humid. Inmates in the older units were allowed personal, clear-plastic electric fans. Special "ice runs" were made to prevent overheating. Large fans were placed on the ranges and in the hallways during the summer. These fans were loud and tended to help conceal abhorrent activities like the sound of sharpening a weapon on the concrete. It is interesting that despite the miserable conditions in the summer, most inmates considered the older single-cell accommodations preferable to the two-man cells in the larger air-conditioned units.

In most of the older units, cell doors were grilles that allowed easy conversation, greater air flow, greater exchanges of items — and, unfortunately, easier opportunity to assault staff. Individual cells were opened by a "lock box," which is a series of large levers at the end of the range — identical to the locking mechanisms that had been used at Alcatraz.

The transition unit allowed greater freedom for the inmates who were housed in it. Instead of access to only the 18 inmates on the range, these inmates were allowed access to everyone in their unit. They all worked together in a small factory inside the prison, and they were allowed to recreate

together and eat together in food service. The goal was to help them transition when they transferred to a less secure facility.

There were very few inmates who were released from the Marion penitentiary to the streets. Most hoped for a transfer to another penitentiary — one that wasn't locked down. Inmates who participated in programming increased their chances of transferring, but it wasn't a sure thing. Some inmates were simply considered too dangerous to be at any other facility.

The difference between inmates in general population and those in SHU wasn't immediately apparent given that everyone was locked in their cells for the majority of the day and SHU cells were secured with grilles as opposed to solid doors, similar to most of the general population units. One major difference was in gaining access to SHU. For general population units, the unit officer would open the door with his key. For SHU, it required coordination between the control center and the SHU officer. Clearly, security was greater for the Special Housing Unit.

In addition, general population and SHU inmates differed in their access to privileges; i.e., general population inmates had a television in their cell, albeit black and white; they could purchase more commissary items; they had more access to the telephone/shower; and they had more

programming opportunities such as participating in education and religious classes via the closed-circuit television system and reading material. In addition, general population inmates could participate in congregate recreation with up to 18 inmates for two and a half hours daily during the weekdays, whereas Special Housing Unit inmates were afforded the opportunity to recreate one hour daily for five hours a week.

With the exception of the 50 inmates who were housed in the transition unit, all inmates were fed in their cells. Special, temperature-regulated food carts were wheeled to each unit three times a day. The officer walked down the ranges and distributed food trays and drinks to the inmates. After thirty minutes, the officer collected and counted the trays to ensure all had been returned, and the carts were returned to Food Service.

Two officers were assigned to each general population unit due to security issues and because these officers had diverse responsibilities. There had been three officers on each unit prior to my arrival at Marion. The downsizing had apparently been recent, given the amount of complaining I heard from staff. Staff safety was always a big concern, as it should have been. However, Marion's complaints paled in comparison to Leavenworth's, given the type of inmates, the staff-to-inmate ratio and openness of the facility.

Officers were constantly present on the unit. In addition, Health Services staff walked each range at least twice every day to tend to medical needs and deliver medication. Commissary staff visited each unit every week to deliver items the inmates bought at the commissary. Case management and religious services staff walked the ranges at least once per week. Each week, all department heads and executive staff walked every range to get a visual of every inmate. In short, inmates had ample access to staff and were at the mercy of staff to ensure their needs were met. You might think this would make inmates feel vulnerable and motivate them to be on good behavior, but you'd be incorrect.

A major difference between the population at Marion and the population at Leavenworth wasn't that Marion had more dangerous inmates. Leavenworth — and, I suppose, the other high-security level facilities as well — had an assortment of inmates who could easily have been interchanged with the inmates who were housed at Marion. They were just as dangerous and had committed the same types of infractions as those in Marion, including staff homicides. The reasons inmates were transferred from other prisons to Marion depended on a lot of different factors, including vacancies. The most common reason was they couldn't be managed at lower-level facilities —

they were impervious to repeated sanctions for misconduct.

The difference between the two populations was the existence of a small subset of inmates at Leavenworth who were motivated to not get into trouble (for varying reasons) along with those who were capable of following rules. There were also inmates who had a more advanced level of emotional maturity. These more adaptive, more conforming inmates contributed unseen assistance in the maintenance and stability within the facility. There were several occasions at Leavenworth when tension was running high between individuals or groups, and these more mature inmates — intentionally or unintentionally — intervened. This intervention involved listening, making rational decisions, making intelligent suggestions, or instituting peer pressure that consequently sometimes restored order — relatively speaking. When inmates complained about their treatment by staff, how they were talked to, a change in cell or unit assignment, there was the opportunity to commiserate with other inmates, which had a calming effect. If the situation related to a small, unpaid debt or a misstep (unintentional disrespect), these inmates might intercede by speaking with the aggrieved. Sometimes, if these inmates were concerned about

the possibility of a serious escalation, they'd quietly advise staff of their information.

At Marion, there was an absence of this type of productive inmate and an absence of his effects on inmate interactions. Often, when an inmate on a range became upset, the rest of the inmates took the opportunity to escalate the situation. They'd chime in somehow, either agreeing with whatever injustice the inmate believed had occurred or yelling insulting and provoking words at him. This would occur for various reasons — sometimes due to boredom or a sadistic urge to see/hear an inmate in distress. Sometimes the provocateurs got vicarious pleasure from watching the involved inmate get riled up to the point he'd assault staff, and sometimes they just wanted a particular inmate moved off the range. If an inmate became too disruptive, oftentimes he'd be moved to another range, unit, or to the Special Housing Unit.

Another unique aspect of USP Marion — until 2007, when the security level changed — was the total absence of illicit drugs. I can't imagine there are many correctional facilities that can make *that* claim. Even residential, substance-abuse treatment centers have contraband. Marion inmates were tested on a frequent (at least monthly) and routine basis. No one ever tested positive for drugs. Of course, the use of homemade alcohol (hooch) was a different story.

The most obvious reason for the absence of drugs at Marion (along with ADX Florence) was the no-contact visiting room. All visits were conducted through glass with the use of a telephone. Unlike most visiting rooms in the Bureau of Prisons — where inmates are allowed to hug their family members, kiss their spouse once at the beginning of the meeting and once at the end, share food/drinks, sit with children on their laps and play games together — there was no opportunity for the exchange of any substances at Marion.

Although open visiting rooms are understandable, this is an often-used avenue for contraband introduction, including drugs, tobacco, and cell phones. There are many inmates' wives serving their own sentence for introducing narcotics through the visiting room. While I was at one of the low-security facilities, a young mother smuggled drugs into the visiting room via her infant's diaper — a story that was more common than one may want to believe.

There's a great deal of attention paid at all facilities to preventing the introduction of contraband. Despite the monitoring of mail, delivery trucks, visitors, and perimeter fence lines, there's always some kind of drug available to inmates at most facilities. This ranges from marijuana to intravenous use of heroin and everything in between. Of course, the inmates pay

more for these substances than they would on the outside, but they're available. While I was at Leavenworth, an inmate was found nonresponsive with a needle still in his arm from a heroin overdose and later pronounced dead.

At many facilities, drugs were unfortunately also brought in by staff who were compromised or greedy. Given that no inmate was ever found to be using or possessing drugs when Marion was locked down, it was a widely accepted fact that Marion had no "dirty" staff when it came to this issue. Marion staff took great pride in this fact.

There were inmates at Marion who had long substance-abuse histories, some of which I'd previously worked with at other facilities. An inmate who'd been in one of the first drug treatment groups I'd facilitated when I was a Drug Treatment Specialist at FCI Seagoville some fifteen years prior was now at the maximum security facility at Marion. I strongly suspected he'd been using heroin while he was in the treatment group, and he'd received an additional sentence for attempting to have his wife smuggle drugs into the prison. He told me drugs and gang affiliation had been his downfall, but he was finally "clean" — not necessarily by his choice. At Marion, there were no drugs to be had. Despite being in a maximum-security prison, these chronic substance abusers looked good. They appeared healthy,

physically strong, and mentally clear. It was a good starting point for making changes if they chose to stay on that path.

After Marion was no longer locked down following its mission change to a medium-security facility in 2007, drugs became abundant — just like in other facilities. There's no doubt the visiting room was the main passageway. Tobacco was also a hot commodity. For tobacco, inmates would go to extremes. It was common for inmates to scavenge for used chewing tobacco. Yes, it's disgusting. They'd dig it out of the trash or try to abscond with a staff member's plastic bottle or soda can spittoon, dry the contents in a microwave oven, and then sell it. Staff were encouraged to pay particular attention to how they discarded their chew.

CHAPTER 4: A Brief History

USP Marion has been open since 1963 — two decades longer as a federal penitentiary than Alcatraz. Alcatraz housed federal prisoners for twenty-nine years (1934-1963). While there are a multitude of books about Alcatraz, there have been only a handful of books written about Marion. Marion was built to be the most secure federal facility in the country at that time. It was the first to have a Control Unit for the most notorious inmates. It was the first USP to be named a supermax. Hence, Marion held the most dangerous criminals in the country.

Understandably, Marion's history consists of dramatic escape attempts including the fabrication of an electronic device that opened the remote-control grilles, an attempt to land a hijacked helicopter in the facility, holding hostages for ransom on a seized airplane at the local airport, and several inmates attempting to climb the fence after shots were fired as a distraction by an accomplice at the tree line. Although the electronic device allowed five inmates to walk out the front door, they were later apprehended and security measures increased. A manual override on all

egresses was installed to keep other clever inmates from manufacturing door-opening devices and an additional tower was constructed to keep inmates from walking out the front door. The female who hijacked the helicopter was killed by the helicopter pilot, who was ex-military and wrestled the gun from her immediately prior to landing at the prison. Wire mesh was installed over the open yard to prevent airborne escape attempts. The female who seized the plane surrendered to the FBI after 10 hours on the runway. The latter two attempts were initiated by the same inmate. He died while incarcerated.

Although USP Marion became known as the institution that replaced Alcatraz, there were, in fact, no inmates who transferred directly from Alcatraz to Marion. Alcatraz inmates were transferred to the handful of federal penitentiaries that were open at the time: Leavenworth, Lewisburg, Atlanta, and McNeil Island. Marion initially housed relatively young and lower-security offenders until the security was tested and proven. In 1964, the first maximum-security inmates arrived. The institution could house around 500 inmates.

For USP Marion staff, the most significant incidents were the murders of three staff members. On January 26, 1969, correctional officer Vern Jarvis was murdered by an inmate and, on October

22, 1983, correctional officers Gene Clutts and Robert Hoffman were murdered at two different times by two different inmates on the same day. As a result of continuing tension between staff and inmates — including an extended food strike by inmates and lawsuits alleging that long-term lockdown conditions were cruel and inhumane — USP Marion became the first prison to be permanently locked down with inmates secured in their cells for most of the day. This was when it became designated as a supermax.

When I transferred to USP Marion in November 2002, it was readily apparent that staff were still very much affected by the officers' deaths nineteen years earlier even though the majority of staff didn't work at USP Marion at that time. Overall, there seemed to be vicarious trauma that was shared throughout the institution. A contributing factor was likely the absence of an understanding in 1983 of the importance of providing crisis support to staff to ease the effects of the trauma. But, more significantly, there seemed to be years of anger and resentment that had developed between labor and management. Correctional officers believed management had been neglectful and hadn't been attentive to staff safety issues. There was a common belief that, during that time period, management consistently ignored and failed to respond to the increasing violence against staff.

The result was a skepticism and anger toward management that escalated and persisted. The fact that the institution didn't lock down following the first murder on October 22, 1983 gives some support to this opinion. It was also significant that Marion exists in an area where there's been intense and sometimes violent labor-management disputes for generations, originating in the coal mining industry. (See Angle, Paul M. *Bloody Williamson.* 1952: Champaign, IL, University of Illinois Press)

During most of my tenure at Marion, there was some degree of tension between management and labor. Depending on the warden's leadership style, this ranged from negligible to extreme. The level of tension seemed to mostly depend on personality styles not on issues. Issues between labor and management in the prison environment were potentially much more significant than in other environments because inmates attempted to capitalize on the rift to compromise safety and security. Inmates used any opportunity to cause dissension among staff members — for personal entertainment, to get someone into trouble, to have someone injured, or to effect an escape.

There were more than a few occasions where inmates would relay to me some comment another staff member had made about me. Or they'd take the opportunity to talk negatively about a staff member, hoping I'd commiserate.

One staff member who worked on a particularly difficult unit was the recipient of a full cup of feces and urine to the face. The cocktail went into his eyes and mouth. The inmate had given no prior indication of feeling animosity toward the staff member. The assault was completely unexpected. As if it was part of the how-to manifesto for creating friction among staff, the inmate convinced the victim that other staff members had caused him to do this. The inmate indicated that his frustration and the subsequent assault were a direct result of specific staff members telling him the victim had tampered with his mail. Thus, not only did the inmate assault the staff with human waste, he caused the victim to become distrustful of coworkers he'd known and depended on for years. He'd been manipulated by a master manipulator — one who knew humans are most vulnerable when trying to make sense of something senseless.

CHAPTER 5: Rules and Regs

Inmates are designated to facilities that match their security level. Security level is determined by many factors including criminal history, institution conduct, sentence length, etc. This is done in the hope of keeping the most dangerous inmates separated from the least dangerous. Inmates work their way up or down security levels. There are transfers from institution to institution when an inmate has a change in their security level, gets into a situation with another inmate that indicates it's no longer safe for him to remain at the same facility, when the BOP has population needs (one facility is overcrowded), or there's an attempt to get the inmate closer to his release destination.

In terms of housing, most facilities assign inmates to cells with at least one other cellmate, or inmates live in a dormitory-style unit. They're allowed out of the cell/unit during the day to work, recreate, eat, and participate in education, religious, and psychology programs. Work consists of cooking or cleaning in Food Service, assisting with services that keep the institution running — i.e., plumbing, electrical, HVAC, washing clothing

and linen — assisting with the commissary (the store that sells a variety of food and toiletries of better quality than those provided to indigent inmates), tutoring in education, monitoring the library, cutting hair in the barbershop, or keeping the institution clean.

The money that inmates are paid comes from a trust fund. The BOP takes money that's generated by the commissary and through MP3 song purchases (yes, inmates can purchase MP3 players) to pay the inmates. Inmates are paid between $.12 and $.40 per hour. The pay may sound like pittance, but keep in mind they don't pay for room or meals. In addition, the majority get money from home.

Most inmates have to make a financial responsibility payment (FRP) comprising restitution and court costs. This is established by the court during sentencing. The monthly or quarterly payment is based on how much money the inmate brings in to his account not on how much he makes by working. Thus, if Mom deposits $1000 in Junior's account every month for six months, that amount is added to the $18.00 he makes each month when calculating his payment. This is sometimes a bone of contention, but it gets the inmate's debt paid.

Federal Prison Industries, also known as Unicor, is a separate inmate work program. When

I started with the Bureau of Prisons, this program was widespread. Almost every institution had at least one factory that produced items such as textiles, cables, printed documents, and furniture. Due to political pressure (stealing business from small privately owned industries), many of these factories have since closed. The cable factory at USP Marion remained viable. Inmates who work in Unicor are paid from the money made from the sale of their products. The inmates are paid between $.23 and $1.15 per hour, thus work in prison industries is usually more prestigious and profitable. The BOP likes to state that these industry jobs help inmates become better citizens and quotes statistics about how these inmates show a much lower recidivism rate, meaning they're less likely to return to prison upon release. What seems to be ignored is the obvious selection bias. Inmates chosen to work in Unicor industries tend to be more mature, better educated, and have little or no history of misconduct during imprisonment.

BOP institutions offer education and recreation opportunities. Inmates without a high school degree are required to work on their GED and put in at least 240 hours toward that training. Inmates who fail to do this are held to lower pay grades and not allowed to work certain jobs. In addition, adult continuing education courses are offered and

inmates have the opportunity to enroll in college courses (at their own expense; however, in the past — and likely in the future — Pell Grants were available). Courses are also offered to teach English to those for whom English isn't their first language. These are predominately Spanish-speaking inmates. There are also arts and crafts, sports, exercise classes, and libraries (both general and legal).

Psychology services offer assistance to those who are mentally ill along with facilitating self-improvement groups such as communication skills, anger management, and cognitive behavior therapy. In addition, inmates can participate in a variety of drug treatment programs, including a 500-hour, intensive residential program. To motivate participation in this program, non-violent inmates can qualify for up to a one-year reduction in their sentence upon successful completion of the program.

There are opportunities for inmates who are interested in self-improvement — to an extent. If an inmate has a higher level of education, advanced knowledge in the fine arts, or a great deal of experience with athletics, there are limited opportunities for growth. I often heard complaints from lawyers, pharmacists, anesthesiologists, and politicians that our services to our more educated inmates were subpar. Most programs cater to those

who have some sort of deficiency and are in need of assistance. It's worth noting that there's a requirement for self-motivation. Most staff encourage inmates to get involved in education, recreation, psychology, or vocational programs, but, unfortunately, the inmates who need the least help are the ones that take most advantage of this opportunity. Often times, institutions attempt to persuade inmates to participate in programming by offering preferential housing (quieter units, larger cells), first in line for meals, later television hours, popcorn, extra movies, etc.

Health services are available, although this is nearly always an area of discontent among inmates. There seems to be a general, underlying suspicion that the health services staff — consisting of physicians, mid-level practitioners, and nurses — aren't qualified or aren't attentive. There's likely numerous reasons for this, including the unfortunate belief by inmates that no competent medical professional would choose to work with inmates. In fact, there are indisputable advantages to working in the federal system including more attractive work schedules and retirement benefits.

At least part of the antipathy toward medical staff occurs because many inmates have limited experience with seeking medical attention or have been incarcerated for a long period of time. They

have lofty beliefs about how quickly a citizen in the outside community gets seen for medical or dental problems. Their expectations are unrealistic.

Overall, the inmate population has above-average medical needs. In large part this is due to neglect of physical/dental health prior to their incarceration, histories of extensive substance abuse, and an aging population. There are excessive medical demands and costs in the BOP. To help alleviate some of the costs, the BOP began requiring inmates to purchase recommended over-the-counter medications at the commissary unless they're indigent, and they're required to pay a nominal copay of $2.00 when they request to be seen. This serves to decrease some of the gratuitous visits to medical services.

According to the Federal Register, the estimated cost to house a federal prisoner in 2014 (the latest figures) was $30,619 annually. Clearly, a lot of money. However, there are several reasons this is a wise investment. Some of the money goes toward keeping the inmates busy: religious programming, recreation, and adult education classes. If inmates aren't kept busy, they're much more likely to engage in nefarious activities, including escape attempts. Some of the money goes to programs to rehabilitate the inmate — again, with education but also through vocational training, sex-offender treatment, and substance-abuse treatment. The

idea is to invest in these individuals while they're incarcerated to increase the likelihood they won't return to prison upon release. Although these programs have been offered for many years, there's really no definitive evidence that they work to lower the recidivism rate. Of course, some of the money — a great deal of the money — goes toward medical treatment, maintenance of the facilities, and staff salaries.

In addition to the expense of housing inmates, there's a large expense involved in addressing lawsuits. The BOP makes a great deal of effort to avoid and resolve lawsuits. It's disappointing how many lawsuits are settled out of court, which, of course, increases the number of lawsuits that are filed. Inmates sue the Bureau of Prisons and staff for nearly anything. Indeed, there are legitimate lawsuits, but they pale in comparison to the many unwarranted suits. An inmate attempted to sue me because he wasn't prescribed medication for a mental illness. This, despite the fact he didn't have a mental illness and I'm not a psychiatrist, therefore I'm not able to prescribe medication. Another inmate attempted to sue me because he was assaulted. I wasn't present at the assault and had absolutely nothing to do with it. Inmates sue, claiming discrimination, loss of property, denied entry into a program they don't qualify for (completion of the program may result in a

sentence reduction), and medical malpractice or negligence, along with allegations of abuse.

CHAPTER 6: Classes, Cuffs and Cameras

I suspect most correctional staff don't fully know what they're getting into when they take employment with the Bureau of Prisons. Of course, everyone knows they'll be working with inmates, but that can mean a variety of different things. There are inmates who "are good people that made a bad decision and got caught." There are substance abusers who wouldn't have committed a crime but for the fact they were addicted. There are inmates who are primarily criminals who have secondary substance-abuse problems — they abuse drugs to enhance their criminal behavior. There are mentally ill inmates ranging from those suffering from schizophrenia to those experiencing mild depression, those with brain damage, those with serious intellectual deficits, and those with sexual deviancy. There are inmates who belong to gangs and process the world from the perspective of the gang. There are those with severe personality disorders and those who are good ol' fashioned psychopaths.

Regardless of the reason for the criminal behavior, as the institution security level increases, the intensity of criminality increases

and vice-versa. Despite this fact, the Bureau of Prisons doesn't allow staff to carry or use any lethal weapons inside the institution unless there are exigent circumstances, such as a riot. Firearms are provided only for security reasons not for safety reasons. Those who work perimeter security or are outside the fence/wall — i.e., those in towers or roving patrols and medical escorts — are issued weapons. Prior to 2015, staff who worked inside the institution were allowed to carry only a radio and a pair of handcuffs for defense. The exceptions were the two supermax facilities, which had been given authorization for staff members to carry batons.

In emergency situations, non-lethal weapons such as gas, foam batons, rubber pellets, and sting ball grenades (a device that releases rubber pellets at a high velocity) can be accessed, but these can't be carried by staff routinely. These are usually used to restore order. During the years I worked for the BOP (1989-2014), there were four staff murders in the federal prison system. All of these occurred during normal operations, not during emergency situations. After the last one, there was a push to allow more access to defensive weapons. Finally, in 2015, the Eric Williams Correctional Officer Protection Act was passed, giving staff the option to carry non-lethal pepper spray at facilities that were medium level or higher.

Most staff expect to have to deal with inmates who misbehave in a variety of ways within the prison. The BOP goes to great lengths to train staff on safety and security issues. Staff attend two weeks of initial training at the facility and then three weeks of training at the Federal Law Enforcement Training Center in Glynco, Georgia. There's an annual refresher training that comprises a forty-hour course including self-defense, CPR, infectious diseases, communication, disciplinary issues, diversity, and firearms training. What isn't addressed is the disparity between inmate and staff rights.

Inmates can assault, swear at, threaten, yell at, spit, throw feces, and ejaculate on staff. They can even place fraudulent liens on staff's personal property, which has long-term, deleterious financial effects. These liens are most popular with a group of inmates called Sovereign Citizens. I cannot even begin to explain this group's anti-government belief system, but their weapon of choice is paperwork. They place liens on government employees' property under the Uniform Commercial Code. Until recently, most states didn't require documents to authenticate the claims. The liens ruin credit ratings and are difficult to resolve.

In response to any of the aforementioned types of misconduct, affected staff can write up a

document called an incident report and submit it to the Lieutenant's Office. That's all. Hopefully, the inmate will be disciplined, which might include a loss of a variety of privileges — from a maximum loss of fifty-four days per year of sentence reduction awarded to inmates for good conduct to loss of commissary benefits, telephone use, email use, visiting privileges, and/or placement in SHU (assuming they aren't already there). Long story short, inmates can be abusive to staff and staff can do very little in response. This is true for all law enforcement officers. Yes, it's part of the job, but, over time, the inequity can take a toll.

From most staff members' perspective, inmates are ungrateful and disgruntled with all services provided and tend to make a habit of grumbling and offering numerous and often inappropriate suggestions for improvement — i.e., access to more prescription medication, more guitars (ignoring the fact that guitar strings are stolen and used to make tattoo needles), additional television channels (they *only* have access to basic satellite television), a greater selection of commissary items (ignoring the fact that not everyone wants the same thing and there's a limited amount of space in the commissary), better food (ignoring the issue of expense and the fact inmates consistently are served better lunches than many public school

children), etc. Of course, as with all populations, you tend to only hear from those who complain.

Despite all the training the Bureau provides, there are situations that occur when staff simply don't know how to react. This is likely caused by a myriad of factors but mostly the unpredictability of human nature. Like most people, staff want to believe they can predict outcomes. If an inmate is upset or has a history of anger problems, he's more likely to engage in an assault. If an inmate is creepy, has been stalking a staff member, or is a sexual offender, he's more likely to act out sexually. But sometimes this just isn't the case and there's no forewarning of what's about to transpire.

When I was at Leavenworth, there was an older inmate who worked with the painting crew. He was polite, quiet, and respectful. He'd recently success- fully painted several staff members' offices in the unit and asked to paint mine. It wasn't unusual for inmates to do extra work around the facility, so I agreed, and he completed the job in a few days without issue. He didn't linger or engage in excessive conversation. He came in, did the job well, and left.

A couple weeks later, while I was monitoring inmates during the noon meal, I was called by a female staff member who was extremely upset. She asked me to come to her department. I arrived as quickly as I could. She was alone and distraught.

She explained that an inmate had just grabbed her and kissed her. When she screamed, he ran off.

He was able to leave her unsecured department and gain access to other areas of the institution unnoticed because of the amount of inmate movement allowed during the noon meal. When units or departments were released for lunch, some inmates went to the recreation yard, some moved from work areas to their cell house, and some went to Food Service for lunch. It looked similar to student movement in the hallways of a high school during lunch.

The staff member explained that the inmate had been painting her office. Yes, the same inmate. I later found out he'd painted six offices before painting hers, and all the offices were occupied by female staff. She was alone in the department with him when he was released for lunch. She decided to lock up the department and go to lunch at the same time. As they walked down the hallway — a hallway that was monitored by a closed-circuit camera — she checked doors to ensure they were secured. At the end of the hallway, there was a small alcove with a door. The inmate asked her if she was going to check that door too. Without thinking, she approached the door, which took her out of view of the camera. That's when the inmate grabbed her.

I'd learned, years before while working as a Drug Treatment Specialist in Seagoville, that it wasn't uncommon for inmates to misinterpret the behavior of female staff. I held group in a room that had a wall of windows that faced the common area yard, which serviced almost every building in the facility. Inmates — who can act very similar to middle-school students — sometimes felt compelled to remark on female staff who walked by. It was fascinating to learn that most male inmates believed the motivation of almost every female on the compound was to gain attention from the inmates. It never occurred to them that these women were secretaries or other staff who were simply doing their jobs, such as going to pick up the department's mail.

So, I suspect the inmate painter misinterpreted the staff member's willingness to walk down the hall with him as her showing an interest in him. He assumed she was going to be receptive to his advances and immediately left when she wasn't. If his intention had been to assault her, he'd have quickly silenced her and continued the assault.

Why had she called me instead of alerting all staff for assistance as she'd been trained? She was a relatively new staff member to Leavenworth and, as odd as it may sound, some new staff members don't want to overreact, so they "under" react. She was likely embarrassed to have ended up in that

situation. She was upset, perhaps stunned, by the whole event, which sounded like it was over as quickly as it began. As I stated earlier, this inmate wasn't someone that would cause you to raise your guard. I immediately notified the Lieutenant's Office. The inmate was located and placed in SHU.

In this case, the inmate was transferred to another facility. Often, if an inmate engages in behavior that might result in staff misconduct — for example, an inmate assaults a female staff member and other staff feel compelled to beat the shit out of that inmate — the administration transfers the inmate to another institution where the situation is less volatile. The inmate is placed in the receiving institution's SHU and goes through the same disciplinary process that would have occurred had he stayed at the previous institution. He'd be issued an incident report, written by the female staff member, and the infraction would be classified as a minor assault. The inmate would likely serve a certain period in SHU and lose good-conduct time. Upon serving his SHU sentence, he'd be released to the new facility's general population and hopefully be given a job where he had limited access to female staff.

CHAPTER 7: Marion's Average Joe

Very few inmates are designated to a maximum-security facility straight from court. The vast majority work long and hard to get there. They're initially designated to a regular facility commensurate with their needs: minimum-, low-, medium- or high-security. At these institutions, when an inmate engages in misconduct, he loses commissary privileges, visitation, telephone, and e-mail, or is placed in SHU for a period of time. Misconduct impacts the inmate's points, which are used to determine his security level. If his points go up (or down, for that matter), he's generally transferred to a facility that matches his newly acquired security level. Transfers occur one level at a time. An inmate that engages in misconduct at a low-level facility transfers to a medium-level facility. If he's at a medium-level facility when the misconduct occurs, he transfers to a high-security facility.

Transfers to Marion when it was a supermax were rare — usually one or two inmates per week. Transfers to Marion as a medium-level facility aren't rare. Usually there's a bus full of inmates going and coming each week. The BOP tries to stay

true to security level points, keeping their institutions pure — which means, if an institution is a medium-security institution, ideally every inmate in that facility has security points within the range of a medium-security facility. If something occurs and his points change — i.e., he serves a percentage of his sentence, causing points to drop or he receives an incident report causing his points to increase — he'll be transferred. Points for incident reports are tallied according to the severity and frequency of the misconduct. Several minor incidents within five years can result in a transfer, but one serious offense may not result in a transfer if the point tally doesn't increase the security level. Misconduct is divided into four levels: 1) low-severity misconduct such as malingering or using abusive language, 2) medium-level severity such as refusing to work or insolence, 3) high-level severity such as fighting or offering a bribe, and 4) highest-level severity such as encouraging a riot or killing.

The majority of inmates at lower-level facilities follow policies and rules. They might engage in minor misconduct but, if they get caught, they usually respond pretty quickly to the disciplinary process and complete their sentences without problems.

Inmates who end up at a supermax either fail to comply with the rules over and over again or

engage in extreme behavior while at a high-security facility. Generally, they have many opportunities to change their future course but choose not to. They're intractable; no matter what privilege is taken from them, they're unaffected. This isn't due to mental illness. They're simply defiant. Their sanctions increase and they work their way up in the system by transferring to higher-security institutions, with the last stop being a supermax. They don't alter their course because the loss of commissary, loss of contact with their loved ones, and increased restrictions on their freedom have no impact on their behavior. These losses are either not that important to them or suffering these losses is worthwhile in some way. The benefit outweighs the cost. You may think there's more to it than this, but there isn't.

There have been lawsuits filed by inmates specifically regarding the negative effects of "solitary confinement," primarily at ADX Florence. I want to remind you, people very rarely end up in a supermax from the get-go. This only happens in the most extreme cases, such as with individuals considered the utmost threat to the community or nation. The vast majority work their way up to it. The average inmate is deterred from misconduct long before he ends up at a supermax. Inmates don't want to be cut off from their loved ones. They realize they won't be able to tolerate the increased

restrictions, so they opt to follow the rules. They realize if they're involved in repeated assaults within one year, they'll lose a great deal and therefore they don't do it.

But inmates who end up at a supermax think and feel differently. They simply aren't impacted by the things that affect you and me. They're not even impacted by the things that affect most inmates.

Inmates housed at Marion supermax tended to fall into two broad categories, although all of them were at the extreme end of being manipulative. They had a disregard for social norms, a penchant for victimizing others, and lacked genuine emotions and empathy. Most had a general arrogance and engaged in pathological lying. The difference between the two groups had to do with the degree of impulse control and emotional lability.

One group tended to be volatile and engaged in extreme and erratic behavior. They needed a great deal of stimulation and were easily bored. Because of their frequent displays of unruliness, there's little doubt they were exactly where they needed to be — confined to a cell.

The other group was glib, charismatic, and appeared earnest and emotionally controlled. They were conversant, intelligent, and interesting. These are the most dangerous beings because

they're so good at what they do. Left to my own devices — i.e., my observations, interviews, or intuition — I could easily believe they weren't dangerous. There's no signal they're lying or insincere. They're consistent in their stories and appearance. They're an amazing breed and fascinating to talk with.

All staff know the best predictor of future behavior is past behavior. The inmates at Marion have a history of violence, manipulating and intimidating others, and/or compromising staff. So it's important to not trust your own senses when it comes to making decisions regarding these inmates.

It didn't take me long to conclude that many of the inmates at the supermax were evil. It was clear a piece of their humanity was missing. I'd worked with evil inmates at every security level, but it was rare, and I didn't recognize it at the time. It was only after being inundated with them and in retrospect that I became aware of this fact.

It's amusing that a common proclamation from this type of inmate is, "I'm not a bad person." In fact, I don't think I ever heard an inmate describe himself as a bad person — even after stabbing another inmate 27 times, talking about raping children or molesting his daughter, committing arson, burning a baby to death, repeatedly extorting the elderly, or abusing his parents. I

never asked their definition of "a bad person." Whatever it was, they never qualified.

I think the expression "banality of evil" fits the population of a supermax perfectly. This expression was originally used to describe Adolf Eichmann and refers to ordinary people who are simple-minded. (Arendt, Hannah. *Eichmann in Jerusalem: A Report on the Banality of Evil*. 1963: New York, Viking Press) But I'm using it to describe the prevalence of evil at USP Marion, which was quite ordinary. The general depth of inhumanity and level of demands, manipulation, hatefulness, and infantile behavior of these inmates were much more saturated than at Leavenworth, although I encountered plenty of it there, too. If you want to know what the average, most troublesome inmates look like, I think Sam Rockwell's portrayal of "Wild Bill" Wharton in the movie *The Green Mile* (1999) was spot on. His energy level and complete disregard for others captures the most common problem for inmates: poor boundaries. There's a general unwillingness to respect other's space, possessions, opinions, or attend to one's hygiene, voice level, or bodily functions.

There was one inmate at Marion, we'll call him T. Marquis, who asked me to get the address of Victoria Gotti, a reality television personality, at the time, and the daughter of deceased Gambino

crime family Mafia boss John Gotti. Normally, this was a needy but polite inmate, at least toward me. He was sent to Marion from a high-security facility after breaking a correctional officer's nose by head-butting her when he was in restraints. The inmate asked me several times to get him Ms. Gotti's address, showing me her book and accusing me of being biased because of her name. I explained I did not and would not provide anyone's address. He immediately became demanding and enraged, outstretching his arms, palm up, and yelling that he'd cut his wrists if I didn't give him what he wanted. The intensity of his emotion was the same as if I'd told him we were going to be harvesting his organs soon. It was ridiculous and extreme, to say the least. I just walked away. He didn't engage in self-harm.

J. Hatch was well known to Marion staff for two reasons, he liked to swallow objects and he frequently announced his intent to suicide. Hatch had a habit of swallowing all sorts of inedible objects, including but not limited to parts off the fire suppression system and light bulbs, but his preference seemed to be prison pens. These are soft, easily bendable pens created to prevent their use as a weapon. Hatch had been the recipient of so many surgeries for swallowing objects that the local hospital advised we only send him out when

there was an emergency or a significant accumulation.

Three weeks after I arrived at Marion, while I was enjoying Thanksgiving dinner with my family, the on-duty lieutenant contacted me because Hatch had declared he was suicidal and needed to be seen by a psychologist. The current Chief Psychologist has been the on-call psychologist for the past year and he certainly was due a break, so I went in. When I arrived, Hatch was standing at the front of his cell. As soon as I approached him, he demanded to know who I was. I explained I was the new psychologist and was responding to his report of suicidal ideation. He was incensed that the Chief had not come to see him and had instead sent a lackey. Hatch made his expectation that he be seen by the Chief extremely clear and berated me for ever existing. It had apparently been his intention to ruin the Chief Psychologist's dinner. I had derailed his plan. He didn't seem to care about, or take any pleasure in, the fact he had successfully interfered with my holiday. The night culminated with Hatch gaining an understanding that the Chief would see him the next day during work hours, and not before. When I became chief, I changed the rules about immediate face-to-face contact with every inmate who did the after-hours suicide beckon.

S. Wesson, who was well known for being filthy and seemingly impervious to his stench, periodically engaged in extreme behavior to get what he wanted. It was amusing that this inmate filed a complaint against me, alleging I forced him to allow me to perform oral sex on him. Per policy, I was investigated and quickly cleared.

Wesson had been in SHU for what he considered to be long enough and wanted to move to one of the new, air-conditioned units. Because of his frequent misconduct of throwing feces at officers, staff disagreed, and he remained in SHU for a while longer.

On one occasion, he was moved at his request to the shower for what staff considered to be a welcome change. Inmates were routinely given a disposable razor while they were in the shower so they could shave. The razors were returned to the officer prior to the inmate being moved back to his cell. However, instead of showering, Wesson used the razor to cut his upper arm down to the muscle. He was moved to Health Services, and I was contacted to assess his suicidality. As soon as I opened the door to Health Services, the stench was apparent. I entered the trauma room to find him fully dressed. He had a full beard and greasy, unkempt hair. It was doubtful he'd showered in months. His request to shower should probably have been questioned from the outset.

When asked about the reason for cutting himself, he stated he wanted to be moved to a new cell. He'd been in a "box car" for his previously mentioned habit of throwing feces at staff. Let me explain what a box-car cell is: Most of the cells had open grilles as opposed to solid doors, but there were a few, special-management cells at the back of the unit that had reinforced plexiglass in the vestibule to prevent inmates from throwing things onto staff or the range. These cells were desirable for inmates that wanted more isolation and a quieter space, but they tended to be hot and weren't desirable for inmates who wanted more interaction. These were the box-car cells. It was like a cell inside a box

Wesson denied any intent to commit suicide and only wanted to change cells. My assessment included the observation that he didn't appear to have a depressed mood. His appetite and sleep patterns were unremarkable. He didn't express any feelings of guilt, shame, or worthlessness. There was no indication of distress or impairment other than his desire to change his housing. He had no support system at home or in the facility. He was a disgusting human being and no one had any regard for him. He had poor impulse control, an inability to regulate his emotions, and seemed to be motivated only by the desire to make himself as comfortable as possible at any given moment. He

was willing to do outrageous things, including injuring himself, to get his way. The dilemma was how to appropriately intervene.

Wesson wasn't suicidal and didn't require a suicide watch. A suicide watch entails placing the inmate in safety clothing inside a special cell above Health Services and having a staff member provide twenty-four-hour observation. Oftentimes, the inmate finds this reinforcing because it gets him out of the Special Housing Unit and provides him with constant attention. For Wesson, it would have been counterproductive to place him on watch, as I didn't want to reinforce his behavior and he didn't need this level of attention.

In considering options, it was clear he shouldn't be in an open-front cell because he assaulted staff and, also, this would likely reinforce future misconduct. At that time, placing an inmate in restraints to prevent self-harm at a non-medical facility was very controversial, and we weren't willing to go there. If he was returned to a box-car cell and accidently ended his life as a result of his attempt to manipulate staff, the BOP would appear negligent and be liable.

Many times, decisions were made only because of fear of lawsuits, and this was one of those times. At other facilities, inmates in this type of situation are often placed in a two-man cell with an inmate who'd alert staff to any attempts at self-harm.

However, no inmates in Marion's SHU celled together prior to 2006. So, my best solution was to take the least deleterious option and have him placed in an open-front cell near the front of the range where he could be more closely monitored by staff.

At the next shift change, the incoming officers moved Wesson back to the box-car cell. Their decision was made for purely selfish reasons, because they didn't want to be the recipient of Wesson's shit-flinging rampages. I certainly can't fault them for that. Soon after the move, Wesson ripped out the stitches in his lacerated arm. Ultimately, he was placed on suicide watch for several days.

Another example of an inmate who had constant interpersonal and boundary issues also had to do with the shower and authorized use of a razor to shave. This was in a general population unit. The inmate cut his arm and was threatening to continue to injure himself because he was angry at another inmate on his range. This was his best attempt to problem-solve. He stood bleeding in the shower and refused to comply with requests to be placed in handcuffs and moved to Health Services.

This inmate had been historically managed by a lieutenant who understood the payoff from providing coffee and tobacco to some inmates with poor emotional control. Of course, this was before

smoking in federal buildings was illegal. The inmate, who was indigent, would usually calm down if provided with these substances. Although some will disagree with this management tool, it's unwise to judge unless you've been in this situation. It worked. It was effective. The alternative would cost a great deal of time and money.

There was pressure on staff to avoid all overtime. When an inmate acted up during morning watch (between midnight and 6:00 a.m.), there were no extra staff to help manage the inmate. If he acted up during evening watch (4:00 p.m. to midnight), there may or may not be a few extra staff members depending on other happenings in the institution. Unfortunately, in some situations, it was easier to appease the inmate.

The central figure in the unit is the correctional officer. The officer is always on the unit and handles the minutiae of running it. When unusual problems occur, they call their direct supervisor, the lieutenant, who generally responds by appearing at the unit. Seasoned lieutenants know the inmates and know which staff members to contact if additional assistance is needed. In this case, the lieutenant knew the inmate, knew he had frequent meetings with psychology, and knew he had to be escorted to Health Services. By policy,

even the most benign injuries had to be evaluated. So, the unit officer, two officers called to escort the inmate, the psychologist, and the lieutenant were all on the unit dealing with the situation.

This particular inmate, who'd created un-necessary drama several times before and had responded positively to the lieutenant in the past, decided to taunt the lieutenant on this occasion. While still in the shower, with the less-than-serious wound, he began bragging to the inmates who were locked in their cells about his expertise in manipulating staff. The shower was located at the beginning of the range, with approximately thirty-two cells within earshot of this inmate. The inmate then stated that the lieutenant was his "bitch."

It was easy to see the inmate was getting to the lieutenant, as he (the lieutenant) started to yell back instead of ignoring the provocations. This ignited the range. Inmate bystanders weren't going to miss an opportunity to fuel a bad situation. Meanwhile, there were two other inmates who lived on the range that were proficient at exhausting staff. They decided to take this opportunity to yell at one another, making childish and violent threats to hurt themselves and one another. The entire scene culminated with the lieutenant being pulled off the range to prevent any unprofessional behavior. Eventually, the range

was calmed, the injured inmate was taken to Health Services, treated, and moved to SHU pending review to be moved to a different range in the unit.

On any given day, this scenario would have had no impact on this very good, seasoned, staff member's mood or behavior. But he was human, and sometimes enough is enough. Fortunately, there were other staff members there to intervene.

Staff tend to look out for one another, especially staff at more established facilities. There's a cohesiveness. Marion was one of those facilities that had a lot of "homesteaders," which means most of the staff don't transfer around. They've worked together for a long time and know each other's proclivities. There are staff who are quicker to engage than others. Some yell at inmates on a daily basis, as a matter of course, but never lose control. Some get flustered quicker. Staff intervene with one another if intervention is needed. Because some staff look out for each other — even after serious mistakes are made — the emphasis is on intervening *before* mistakes are made. A preventive intervention is the best intervention.

CHAPTER 8: Hunger Game

Inmates can be very stubborn and believe themselves to be entitled. One of the more challenging problems for prison administrations that inmates have created over the years is the hunger strike. The decision to quit eating is usually to protest some perceived wrong or to manipulate a transfer. In most of these cases, the vast majority of inmates don't make it through a single day without eating. However, there are those few that can.

When an inmate declared himself on hunger strike, a member of the psychology department — often me — first assessed him for mental illness. During this evaluation, I'd discuss with the inmate his concerns and goals. Most of the time, I was familiar with the inmate because he had a history of being problematic to staff at a variety of different levels; i.e., demanding, inflexible, and engaging in general misconduct. I'd usually take this opportunity to encourage alternate means of problem solving and educate him about the BOP's policy on hunger strikes, including the procedures on nasogastric feedings.

Inmate N. Marks, who'd been placed in SHU a few days prior, declared a hunger strike because the SHU property officer hadn't given the inmate his property. When an inmate is placed in SHU, the unit officer packs up and inventories the inmate's personal property in a green duffle bag. The officer then has the bag moved to SHU, where the SHU property officer goes through the contents with the inmate and issues minimal, authorized property such as basic toiletries, a few pictures, letters, stamps, and reading material. Normally, this will occur within three days. If several inmates are placed in SHU at the same time — especially if they all come from one unit — the procedure can take longer. If the Special Investigative Services department needs to look at the property or the FBI wants to look at it, the process can take much longer.

In the case of Marks, he was simply impatient. We discussed how his behavior wouldn't hasten the process. At the conclusion of our conversation, Marks maintained he was going to hold out and not eat. However, he consumed his evening meal.

Inmate N. Jones was a known pedophile and had been repeatedly sanctioned for making intricate collages of children by cutting and altering magazine pictures. Staff sanctioned him to a loss of personal property for 14 days. His personal property consisted of his magazines, pictures, and

personal fantasy-game material (Dungeons and Dragons). Jones declared a hunger strike to protest his treatment by staff. He claimed we were being "cruel and inhuman." He and I had several conversations during the five days he refused to eat regarding his frustration and the consequences of his behavior — both short-term and long-term — but mostly about how his starving himself didn't hurt staff at all. Jones began eating on his own before medical intervention was necessary.

When I say these inmates aren't mentally ill, I want you to understand what I mean. They're in control of their behavior and able to make an informed choice. Their behavior isn't motivated by a delusion or hallucination. They aren't depressed and using starvation as a means to end their life. This is the adult version of a young child holding his breath to get what he wants.

On the rare occasions when an inmate is truly mentally ill, a different course of intervention is applied. Fortunately, I was successful in convincing these inmates to take psychiatric medication, which resolved the eating issue. I'm sure this isn't always the case at medical institutions that house the more severely mentally ill. I wasn't confronted with inmates who were docile or catatonic. In every case, they were agitated at some level due to a delusion or a misperception and had recently discontinued

taking their prescribed antipsychotic medication. The agitation makes it easier to gain compliance as long as there's good rapport. It just takes convincing the individual that the medication will help with their emotional discomfort. They consent to an injection, and the hunger strike falls by the wayside.

Inmates at Marion who declared a hunger strike were almost always residents of SHU. Inmates who were disruptive and ended up in SHU were more likely to attempt to manipulate staff. Hunger strikes were their last-ditch effort. If the inmate wasn't in SHU when he declared the hunger strike, he was by the end of the shift. If the inmate was on the compound (not in SHU) when he announced his intention to hunger strike, a staff member would notify the Lieutenant's Office, and the lieutenant would have the inmate escorted to SHU as soon as convenient. If the proclamation was made when there was a lot of inmate movement, such as during a meal, the order to place the inmate in SHU would be delayed until the halls were clear. The inmate would either go about his business until then or be told to sit outside the Lieutenant's Office until arrangements could be made to walk him to SHU. The inmate was placed in SHU to better monitor his food and water intake. After an inmate refused to take any food from his tray for a duration of nine meals, medical staff began to closely monitor him

to ensure he wasn't risking serious self-harm. Inmates could be very creative when it came to getting food without obviously taking it off their tray, including wrapping items in plastic and using the sewer system to pass food down to adjacent cells from toilet to toilet.

When, or if, it was determined the inmate was putting his health at risk, the inmate was brought to Health Services and fed through a nasogastric tube at least every other day until he resumed feeding himself. When Marion was a supermax, this required a "forced cell" team to move the inmate to Health Services, per policy. A forced cell team is required any time there's a need for a calculated use of force. In this situation, the inmate was considered extremely noncompliant and potentially dangerous.

Per policy, forced cell teams comprise at least five correctional staff donning heavy protective gear including helmets and pads; a medical staff member; a staff member to video-record the entire move and procedure; a staff member to serve as the confrontation-avoidance member (a negotiator); and a lieutenant. The five correctional staff each has a specific role to play if the inmate resists, i.e. one focuses on the torso, one restrains the upper left appendage, one the lower left appendage, etc. The medical staff is present to check for any injuries to the inmate after restraints are applied,

and the videographer is there to protect against lawsuits. The lieutenant is the supervisor in charge. All these staff are pulled from their regular duties to participate. The procedure usually takes ninety minutes to two hours. It's worth noting that the staff who serve on the forced cell team must stand in full gear for the entire duration of the prisoner's out-of-cell movement. In the summer, temperatures in the facility could reach a hundred degrees; with a helmet and pads on, it would be even hotter. I was involved in many cell team moves as the negotiator.

When the move was over and these team members were finally able to remove their gear, it was clear how hot and uncomfortable it must have been to stand motionless for hours with that gear on. I always felt bad for the officers. They'd stand silently while the inmate spoke on and on into the video-recorder about how he was being mistreated. The video was always reviewed by the executive staff of the institution and the correctional services administrator in the regional office. From the length and intensity of some of the inmates' discourses, I'm sure they believed they were speaking directly to the Director of the BOP.

After an inmate on hunger strike was moved to Health Services, he'd be offered a nutritional supplement to drink before the nasogastric procedure. If he refused the drink, a tube was

inserted into his nose, swallowed by the inmate, and then advanced into the stomach. The nutritional supplement was poured into the tube and traveled down by gravity. Inmates rarely struggled during this procedure, knowing there was an increased likelihood of pain or injury if they did.

There are now regulations about the thickness of the tube that can be used for nasogastric feedings to minimize the degree of discomfort. Minimizing the degree of discomfort increases the likelihood the inmate will continue with his protest. There are inmates who continue hunger strikes for months, not because they're mentally ill or being mistreated but because they're simply recalcitrant. Unfortunately, they eventually get their way. They're transferred to another facility where the whole process starts again. Prior to the restriction on tube size, there were some medical staff who would, without causing harm, use a larger tube, making the procedure much more uncomfortable. As you might imagine, most inmates would end the hunger strike after the first feeding.

It's worth noting here that there were and are numerous sanctioned avenues to wage a genuine complaint without declaring a hunger strike. At an informal level, department heads and executive staff are available to speak with inmates at the

noon meal. This is called "standing mainline." All facilities expect a representative from each department to be available during the noon meal, Monday through Friday. If a real problem is brought to staff at that time, it's usually addressed. If there's an allegation regarding abuse by a staff member, the problem is *always* addressed. Even if the allegation is ridiculous, it's still investigated.

Complaints by inmates at Marion included valid concerns regarding medication issues, housing issues (wanting to move to a different cell or unit), inmate pay, job changes, laundry or inmate uniform problems, problems with MP3 players, wanting different television channels, education or recreation hours of operation, etc. They also included amusing concerns such as only being issued two rolls of toilet paper per week or not being able to take fruit from food service (used to make hooch). For inmates who weren't able to eat in the dining hall (as was the case in supermax facilities or inmates in SHU), staff walked the units at least once per week. Inmates were encouraged to talk with staff about their issues then.

The BOP also has a formal administrative remedy procedure in which inmates file complaints to the department head, warden, regional office, and central office. If the complaint isn't resolved at any of these levels, the inmate can use the court system. In addition, inmates aren't shy about

contacting their congressional representatives, who always follow up with the facility to ensure appropriate treatment.

I was contacted twice via a congressional letter regarding an inmate whose mother wanted him moved to a medical facility where he could receive electroconvulsive therapy (ECT) for depression. The inmate frequently had contact with his mother and convinced her of this need. The inmate had been diagnosed with depression prior to incar- ceration and was prescribed an antidepressant. He was given special permission to continue taking that medication while incarcerated, but he refused to take it. Despite this, he functioned relatively well in the institution, with the exception of working. He claimed he was too depressed to work. However, his hygiene was good, he ate meals in Food Service, and frequented the recreation yard. There was no indication his depression had risen to the level of needing ECT — and certainly no need to transfer him to a medical facility.

CHAPTER 9: Use of Force

Cell extractions are used when it's necessary to remove an inmate who isn't cooperative from his cell. If the situation doesn't require an immediate use of force — such as in a serious medical emergency — a forced cell team is assembled and the inmate is moved in a careful, calculated manner to minimize the risk of harm to staff. The frequency with which these are required waxes and wanes depending on the security level of the institution and the general mood of the inmates on any given day. When Marion was a supermax, use-of-force incidents ranged from several in one day to one per month.

The largest undertaking of this type that I witnessed was when a range of eighteen uncooperative inmates had to be moved. This happened on two separate occasions. These teams consisted of five officers who moved the inmates, a lieutenant to lead the move and ensure adherence to policy, medical personnel, a confrontation-avoidance member, a person to run the video camera, and an additional staff member who was there to use less-than-lethal munitions, if necessary. On the first occasion, a gang member

who was housed on a range with several members of the same gang was reassigned to a cell on a different range. Staff wanted his cell for another inmate. These decisions were made for a variety of reasons, but, as mentioned earlier, they were never made lightly. On this occasion, the inmate was to be relocated to the lower tier on the same side of the unit. He would no longer be able to recreate with the same inmates, but he would easily be able to communicate with them. Staff felt this was a good compromise, knowing he wanted to remain near his people, yet knowing that his current cell was the only place the other inmate could be housed safely.

Usually, inmates cooperated during these moves. They were told they'd be moving, they'd pack their belongings, the officer would return to their cell after a few hours, they'd comply with orders to be placed in hand restraints, the grille door was opened, they were escorted to their new cell, the cell door was closed, and the restraints were removed.

When this particular inmate was told he'd be moving, he demanded to know the reason and stated it wasn't happening. On a good day, this inmate might be convinced to cooperate with either a move to the new cell in the unit or a new cell in SHU. Unfortunately, on this occasion, the situation became complicated when the other gang members

on his range decided to rally on his behalf. I suspect they thought the administration wouldn't want the hassle and would just leave the inmate on the range. Not so.

When I arrived as the designated negotiator, the inmates were very clear in communicating through words and tone that there would be no negotiation. The range was noisy as I entered the unit but became eerily silent when the grille was opened for me to enter the range. The floor of the catwalk (the concrete walkway used to access the cells) was covered with water, soap, oil, a variety of food items, and empty containers. Forearms were outside the grilles, with hands holding small, rectangular, reflective items that were used to see who was walking in. I walked to the middle of the range and attempted to talk to the inmate who was refusing to move. He was stern and terse, adamant that he wasn't moving. He glowered and wouldn't answer questions, even benign ones such as, "What's going on?" On my way out of the unit, I stopped at the third cell and tried to interact with an inmate who had some "juice" on the range and with whom I had a rapport. He also glowered and indicated he wasn't interested in talking to me. It was clear there was no way for a positive resolution in which everyone would save face. I knew it would be a long night.

After I left, the inmates continued to throw items onto the range and were hunkering down for battle. They padded themselves with extra clothing, covered their cell bars with blankets to block the view, and put additional water and soap on the concrete floor to impede any type of traction for staff.

Two separate teams were assembled and alternated entering the unit, taking control of one inmate at a time and moving the inmate to SHU. The inmates opted to struggle and fight with the extraction team despite the odds of five to one. Both teams were exhausted by the end of the night, and one staff member was injured, but the job got done.

On the second occasion, inmates who were single-celled in SHU had to be doubled up to make room for several inmates who'd created a serious disturbance on the recreation yard. The SHU inmates refused to cooperate. They used their mattresses and extra clothing to barricade themselves into the corners of their cells. Rubber pellets were shot at cell walls and ceilings to encourage compliance, the intention being that the ricocheting pellets would hit their targets. By the time the team got to the last inmates, there was quiet compliance. An inmate would signal to the staff he'd comply by lying face down on the bed with his hands behind his back. It was important the other inmates not know about the compliance,

because that would be considered a serious betrayal. Job well done.

Occasionally, inmates continue to be assaultive or destructive even after placement in SHU. They spit on, throw feces or urine on, or throw food, food trays, or books at anyone passing by their cells. They might grab or hit a staff member if/when a staff member got too close to the cell. They might destroy institution clothing or mattresses or break the fire suppression system (sprinkler head) in the cell.

If there is no other way to gain compliance and ensure no one is harmed, inmates are placed in progressive restraint. This starts with ambulatory restraints in which the inmate has limited use of his hands but can still move around his cell. At most facilities, the next and final step is called four-point restraints, where an inmate is fastened to his bed by his wrists and ankles. His movement is greatly restricted, but he's able to roll slightly from side to side. The decision to place an inmate in progressive restraints is never taken lightly. And, as soon as an inmate indicates he's calm and agrees to behave, the restraints must be removed, by policy. I believe staff generally abide by this. The exception is when an inmate is clearly just saying what the lieutenant wants to hear and has every intention of becoming assaultive as soon as he becomes free. Inmates in progressive restraints

require a great deal of staff time, paperwork, and notifications to the regional office.

At Marion, there was an additional level of restraints called "the iron cross." The iron cross consisted of the inmate lying on his back on a mattress atop a concrete slab with his arms fully outstretched to the sides. His hands and feet were secured tightly to metal rings embedded in the concrete. This restricted the inmate's movements in such a way that he was unable to change position.

At other facilities, a restraint chair was sometimes used to increase the level of restriction. These chairs are marketed to prisons and are equipped with locking wrist, waist, shoulder, and ankle devices to control violent inmates. Inmates that were able to free themselves from the restraint chair weren't able to free themselves from the iron cross. An inmate in iron-cross restraints was under constant supervision by an officer and checked every two hours by a lieutenant and twice each shift by medical staff. The iron cross was rarely used and only in the most extreme situations.

One of the more unfathomable situations involved a Mariel Boatlift Cuban inmate. There weren't too many remaining in the system by 2004. The Immigration and Naturalization Service (INS) and Immigration and Customs Enforcement (ICE) had slowly released nearly all the Mariel Cubans.

This inmate hadn't been at Marion long. He had very brief periods of behaving and much longer periods of extreme misbehavior. We'd been in contact with INS/ICE, which was trying to place the inmate with his family in Miami. The family was ambivalent. It just so happened that his ICE caseworker finalized his release plans at the same time that the inmate had been engaging in extremely violent behavior in the institution. In his relatively short history at Marion, he'd repeatedly spit on staff, thrown food trays and feces/urine at staff, and attempted to grab staff. He'd spent most of his time in SHU box-car cells or in ambulatory or four-point restraints. When these types of restraints are determined to be ineffective, inmates can be placed directly on the iron cross without going through the increasing progression of restraints each time. For this inmate, the only thing that seemed to get his attention was the iron cross.

Despite the extreme difficulty in managing this inmate, he was scheduled to be released from prison soon, although we didn't know exactly when. The executive staff thought he'd respond favorably to this news, so he was escorted to the part of the institution known as Receiving and Discharge. Here he was told the good news and allowed to pack up his property. The inmate knew this made no sense, because — well, it didn't. An inmate who's

been held for years in a federal prison by Immigration Services doesn't all of a sudden get released, especially after consistent heinous behavior. So he continued his regular pattern of spitting on and threatening staff.

What a paradox for the administration. This man was slated to be released from custody and returned to the community within days. However, his misconduct couldn't be ignored. Doing so ensured risk to the safety of staff. The administration opted for safety and control of the inmate. He was restrained on the iron cross, where he remained for several days because he refused to comply with orders to not assault staff.

ICE contacted us to let us know they wanted the inmate immediately released. Staff entered the cell, informed the inmate — who was still in iron-cross restraints — that he was to be released. They unrestrained him, allowed him to take a shower, gave him some street clothes (jeans and a shirt), and escorted him to the front of the prison.

The inmate refused to leave. I suspect he was concerned that his release was a ruse to make it look like he was escaping and justify having him shot by one of the perimeter officers. It took over an hour to convince him to walk out of the building. To make matters worse, ICE lacked an understanding of this inmate's needs in transitioning to the community.

The release plan was to take this man — who had poor coping skills, limited English, and had been in a highly structured and controlled environment for years — and put him in a transport vehicle that would drop him off at the front of Lambert Airport in St. Louis, Missouri with a plane ticket to Miami. The inmate thought the plan was to drive him to Miami. We can only imagine his confusion. He became highly agitated when he was dropped off at the airport, began pacing and talking loudly, and made other travelers nervous. When security attempted to intervene, he became assaultive and was immediately placed in a county jail where he remained for more than a year. The county jail was a temporary holding facility. Once it was determined there wouldn't be additional charges filed regarding his antics at Lambert Airport, he was returned to an appropriate federal facility — Marion. And he wasn't happy to be back.

CHAPTER 10: The Unusual and Extreme

I actually hate it when someone — usually a politician — uses a specific singular instance to make a point, as if it applies to a much larger population. I want to be clear, the following examples don't represent the mainstream of prison life. They were unusual and extreme. However, I'm positive there are similar examples at every high-security facility in the BOP. This chapter presents four specific vignettes to: 1) highlight how complicated the relationship between inmates and staff can be; 2) describe how unbelievably physically disgusting inmates can be; 3) describe how unbelievably emotionally disgusting inmates can be; and finally, 4) convey how much this can change a staff member's perspective.

The Case of A. Burnett

I knew A. Burnett when I was at Leavenworth. He was memorable for me, more so than Thomas Silverstein. Silverstein was well known in the BOP as one of the two inmates who'd killed two officers in two separate incidents at Marion in 1983 and had a history of killing inmates in prison. I talked

to Silverstein a few times while at Leavenworth. He had his own wing in the Special Housing Unit, separate from everyone else. He had no contact with any other inmates and had limited contact with staff. During my interactions with him, he was polite and nondescript — other than looking like one of the members of the ZZ Top rock band.

A. Burnett, on the other hand, loathed me the entire time I was at Leavenworth — and loathe may be an understatement. I have no idea what led to his feelings toward me, although, based on the content of his orations, it involved some racial tension. The first interaction with him that I recall was being yelled at to get away from his cell door. Burnett was in SHU housing the entire time I was at Leavenworth. He could bang on the door and yell longer and louder than any person I've ever known. From the moment he knew I was in the SHU, which was frequently, until the time I left, he'd yell endlessly about what he was going to do to me, my children, and anyone I knew. It primarily involved severing body parts and sticking those parts into different orifices. He yelled so loudly I couldn't interact with anyone on his range and had difficulty hearing even while on other ranges.

Most staff just accepted this behavior and, eventually, I did too. But initially, me being human and all, it was confusing and bothersome. I'd done nothing to him to warrant any harsh feelings let

alone something so extreme. I wouldn't say it kept me up at night, but I'd be lying if I said it wasn't disquieting. Staff and inmates alike hated it, but there could be no intervention. What could I do? I tried a few times to get him to interact at a meaningful level so I could understand the problem. It was quickly evident that this irritated him even more. Burnett's behavior went on for months. Then, on one occasion, when the orderlies (inmates who were in SHU for misconduct but were allowed onto the range to clean) were out on the range, the control officer mistakenly opened Burnett's cell door, giving the orderlies access to Burnett. Nothing actually happened other than Burnett getting very quiet... for maybe a week. Inmates knew staff had a duty to keep them safe and assumed this would always be the case. Sometimes they needed to be reminded that staff members might not always take their responsibilities seriously or inmates might be at the mercy of someone who makes a mistake.

Several years after I transferred to Marion, who should show up but A. Burnett. I was required to see him for an intake screening. Given that Leavenworth's SHU cell doors were solid, I never really felt threatened by him there. But Marion's SHU doors were grilles. I don't mind telling you it was one of the few times I was a little scared to talk with an inmate. It was also probably the only time

I asked an officer to be by my side during an interaction. Now, don't get me wrong. There were a lot of times that officers were there with me. They were there because of their concern or their knowledge, but I'd never felt that I needed it or requested it.

When I walked onto the range, Burnett looked at me from his cell and smiled. It was like we were best friends. He asked how I was doing and how my husband was doing. This phenomenon of feeling very comfortable and close with staff, which I later found out isn't uncommon, occurs with inmates who do a lot of time and get transferred around. They, like most people, enjoy being with people who are familiar. There's also some prestige that comes from knowing staff members for a long time; i.e., "I knew the warden when he was an officer." During the entire time he was at Marion, Burnett was never disrespectful toward me. He and I talked on several occasions — but we never reminisced about Leavenworth.

The Case of L. Hernandez

There were numerous inmates who would throw feces and urine on staff — females, wardens — it didn't matter. If an inmate doused a staff member with waste material, there was little to nothing that would/could be done. The inmate would be

moved to SHU, but oftentimes they were already there. They could be placed at the back of the range in one of the box-car cells, which would prevent things from being thrown on staff walking by, but this offered little protection to officers who had to deliver meals or escort for recreation or showers, or to medical staff who had to provide medical attention.

I never had feces or urine thrown on me. However, it happens to staff too often. When I've questioned inmates about this behavior, they act as if it's just a normal part of problem resolution. What was even more interesting is how many staff accept this behavior as part of the job. Having feces thrown on you by adults is just part of the job? It's also, somehow, a badge of honor, like surviving a hazing. I suppose that's one of the few ways such an assault could be reframed into something tolerable.

Of the inmates who used feces as his weapon of choice, the most memorable one for me was a Mexican national, Hernandez, who had a terminal medical condition, was due to release soon, and had no prospect of financial resources or social support on the outside. This inmate was a small, quiet individual who was ordinarily pretty cooperative. However, a couple of years prior to his anticipated release date, he began to have periodic meltdowns consisting of insolence and minor assaults. We

suspected he didn't want to be released. He was receiving very expensive medication (thank you, taxpayers) and wouldn't be able to afford these drugs when he was deported to Mexico.

On one occasion, Mr. Hernandez had been placed in a suicide-watch cell due to concerns he might engage in self-harm. He was reassessed a little later and determined not to be in need of the special observation cell and was to be returned to SHU. Prior to the move, he protested by smearing feces all over the walls. I was contacted to help talk Hernandez into cooperating with being placed in restraints and moved to SHU.

To get to the suicide-watch area, which was above the Health Services unit, I walked into the hospital waiting room, took a right through the metal door, went up a flight of stairs, through another metal door, took a right, went through another metal door, and entered M Unit. Mr. Hernandez's cell was halfway down on the right. I was still in the stairwell when I became acquainted with a smell I couldn't have ever imagined. I continued up the stairs and opened the second metal door. I was literally pushed backwards by the odor as in I reflexively stepped back out the unit. The smell was like a mixture of feces, a decomposing body, and an old, used feminine product. The smell must have had something to do with his immune deficiency and whatever was

killing him. It was as if he was rotting from the inside. I did my best to proceed into M Unit. The captain, who was standing in M Unit, turned and looked at me. He knew when he looked in my eyes that I just couldn't handle it. I retreated and waited in the hallway outside of M Unit. I'm not sure what I was waiting for — perhaps to be ordered to do my job or to be sure the task would be completed by some kind soul so I wouldn't *have* to do my job. The smell was overpowering, but, at that distance, at least I could hold my sleeve over my nose and breathe out of my mouth. Eventually, the captain convinced Hernandez to cooperate and he was moved to SHU.

I later found out the captain's olfactory sense was impaired. He couldn't smell anything. I have no idea how the other officers on the unit were able to tolerate the smell. It was quitting time when this occurred, so after I knew the inmate was moved, I went home. I put Vicks VapoRub under my nose and immediately washed my clothes. It was interesting how long the rancid smell clung to my brain.

The Case of S. Coon

Although I suspect most correctional staff don't acknowledge the positive attributes of inmates, I found almost all inmates had some redeeming

value, however slight: a good sense of humor, well-read, articulate, artistic, good social skills, likeable personality (when not criminalizing), etc. S. Coon had absolutely nothing of value. He was slight of stature but didn't have a mouth to match. He constantly pressed for unending attention and was frequently threatening, highly manipulative, and very taxing on staff. He had constant, unreasonable demands and no willingness to begin to address his chronic misconduct or even admit to any issues he needed to address. There was nothing likable about him. He was neither smart nor dull; he didn't read; he wasn't witty; there wasn't an ounce of kindness in him; he had no sense of humor; he wasn't attractive, and he wasn't engaging.

The depth of his malignancy became abundantly apparent during a monitored telephone call. Coon was allowed to make occasional phone calls to his elderly father. On this occasion, he was speaking with his father for the last time. He was aware his father was on his deathbed. His sisters had contacted the chaplain so Coon could speak with his father one last time.

Coon had no money in his account. He couldn't pay for the telephone call, so the chaplain had him escorted to the staff office where he could speak with his father without having to pay. The chaplain and I were present. His oldest sister answered the telephone and held the phone to their father's ear

so Coon could speak to him. He immediately began talking to his father about how he needed money. That was his only message. When the oldest sister got back on the line, he began demanding she send him money. When she refused, he talked to the next sister, with the same demand and result. The conversation culminated with him talking to his youngest sister. As bad as it was, it got worse. He yelled at her that she just needed to get over the fact he'd sexually assaulted her, because that had occurred years ago and he needed money. Indeed, he'd been prosecuted years before for molesting his youngest sister. He never received any money from them.

The Case of L. George

Over time, working in this environment takes its toll. Of course, I became more jaded and cynical. I'm also aware I'd allowed inmates' values and code of conduct to invade my value system, and I can tell you exactly when that awareness occurred. After I transferred to Marion, I heard about an inmate who was murdered at Leavenworth. George was a white inmate and was murdered on the unit by black inmates. Rarely would something like this occur — a murder across racial lines — without it having a large-scale impact on the institution. Things like this can create an enormous amount of

racial tension, but this had not. Apparently George had publicly disrespected an older, well-liked black inmate. Instead of immediately retaliating, the black inmates followed accepted prison decorum and went to the "influential" white inmates. The white inmates indicated they'd handle the situation. George would get a "beat down" and the end result would be George apologizing to the inmate he'd disrespected. George not only refused to apologize, he continued to be disrespectful. Ultimately, the white inmates sanctioned the black inmates to "handle it," and George was killed.

When I heard the story, I listened attentively and then thoughtfully concluded, "Well, everything had been tried to get him to apologize, so he deserved to die." I immediately caught myself. Who was I? How had I become so hardened? I'd always believed in the death penalty, but this was the first time I'd thought a person should be killed for merely disrespecting someone.

CHAPTER 11: Special Housing Unit (SHU)

Criminals don't stop being criminals just because they're in prison. Many continue to overstep the line, creating disruption in what should be a structured environment. There has to be a means for correctional staff to manage these inmates, hold them accountable, and ensure they don't engage in misconduct or harm. This is a particularly challenging task when there are a multitude of restrictions and limits on staff behavior. Many of these restrictions are imposed to protect inmates, but they also limit management options for correctional staff.

There are currently sweeping concerns about all types of law enforcement officers abusing their authority, which has led to the recent trend of police officers wearing cameras and prison staff needing to justify all that they do. Although there is clearly a benefit to this, there must be a balance. Two inmates got into a fight in food service during the evening meal. The altercation was witnessed by numerous inmates. Two staff members broke up the fight by restraining the inmates. The inmates had injuries as well as one of the staff members. Despite the documented injuries and the staff

members report, the incident was disregarded because the camera in the area wasn't working effectively. Since there was no clear video, the fight couldn't be substantiated. No one was held accountable.

Placement of inmates in SHU gained a great deal of attention a couple years ago following the onslaught of lawsuits that resulted in a six-month, independent assessment of restrictive housing programs in the Bureau of Prisons (Federal Bureau of Prisons: Special Housing Unit Review and Assessment, CNA Analysis & Solutions, December, 2014). In prison, SHU is a way to put the imprisoned in jail. It's no different than arresting someone in the community and placing him in the county jail, except the dimensions are much smaller. When someone breaks certain laws in the community, he's separated from law-abiding citizens and sometimes sentenced to jail time. When someone breaks certain rules in the BOP, he's separated from the rest of the population and often sentenced to spending a certain period of time in SHU. Depending on the severity of the offense and its repetitiveness, this ranges from fifteen days to six months. Of course, time can add up if the inmate continues to misbehave while in SHU just like it can add up while a person continues to break rules while in jail.

Inmates are expected to follow these rules: no drugs, no tobacco, no drinking, no tattooing, no fighting, no assaulting, no self-harm, no insolence to staff, no gambling, no stealing, no engaging in illegal activity, no contacting any unauthorized individuals, no public displays of masturbation, no sex with others, no operating businesses, no circumventing security, and no contraband (anything not authorized by the warden, issued by the institution, or sold in the commissary). Inmates are also expected to work, wear their clothes appropriately (no sagging pants), keep themselves and their cells clean, be where they're supposed to be, and stand during daily counts twice per day and three times on weekends.

Most inmates can live within these limits. If someone falters, they usually respond well to BOP sanctions such as loss of sentence reduction opportunities or phone, visitor, or commissary privileges; or experiencing a brief stay in SHU. They get the message after the first infraction or two. But there are those inmates for whom the BOP's sanctions aren't a deterrent. The inmates who spend a great deal of time in SHU are those who continue to break the rules, just like those who repeatedly break the law in the community. To intervene in this cycle, inmates in SHU are given additional encouragement to learn alternative means for problem solving and managing impulses,

anger, and inappropriate behaviors. They are provided reading material, worksheets and interaction with psychology, education and religious services. Some genuinely strive to address their issues and are able to spend longer periods on the compound with no misconduct. Some pretend to work on self-improvement and some are very clear they're not interested.

For those inmates who aren't fazed by SHU or any other restrictions and continue to engage in disruptive behavior, staff have to get creative. Most do this by imposing logical, albeit unofficial, consequences. The problem comes when complaints are made by inmates and only half of the story is told. Staff are given tools to manage inmates, but sometimes the allowed tools fail — over and over and over again. Thus, out of frustration or necessity, staff bend the rules. Unfortunately, when complaints are made by inmates and only half the story is told, it can give the appearance of wanton capricious behavior.

Inmates in SHU who have bad habits such as flooding the cell/range by clogging the toilet get their water temporarily turned off. Inmates who break the fire suppression system in the cell to allow filthy cold water to pour out of the sprinkler head aren't immediately removed from their cell. If an inmate in SHU throws his food tray on the range, he may not get fed at the next meal. If he

throws feces on a staff member, he may have to make do without any property (bedding, toiletries) for a brief period.

When inmates present their tales of woe — of not being fed, of being left in a wet cell, or not provided with clean linens — it can sound like they're being arbitrarily targeted, mistreated, and abused. At one time, had I been the recipient of this information, I'd certainly have concluded the same thing. But, in all honesty, knowing the full story changes the perception.

Furthermore, you may think inmates who engage in these types of behaviors are acting out in response to some great injustice. If there is, it's never made clear. Sometimes inmates complained they wanted to go to recreation that day but hadn't been allowed. Inmates said they wanted to see the captain or the warden that day and the officer wouldn't make it happen. They complained that the counselor or medical staff they wanted to see didn't walk the range on that particular day.

The reasons are varied, but the theme is the same. Something occurs that's perhaps justifiably upsetting and, because they don't get their way, they feel compelled to overreact in an effort to regain some power or control. Sometimes, after the fact, I'd talk to them and they'd see the error of their ways. We'd discuss alternatives and more adaptive ways to handle their frustrations.

But then another perceived slight occurs, their maladaptive behavior recurs, and the officer handles it in the aforementioned ways. It's usually an effective management tool.

Every week, all inmates in SHU are reviewed by a committee that includes the warden, associate warden, captain, SIS (investigation staff), unit managers, case managers, health services, and psychology staff. The goal is to ensure that all inmates housed in SHU are there for good reason; i.e., waiting to be disciplined, serving out their SHU sentence, in protective custody, or unable to be on the compound for a variety of reasons ranging from a potential conflict of interest in interacting with a staff member they knew in high school to recovering from an injury. If an inmate doesn't belong in SHU — and sometimes even if he does — an effort is made to get him out of that unit as soon as possible.

There are inmates who choose to languish in SHU. They prefer to be there and refuse to leave. This can be because they prefer the solitude, they're generally afraid, they owe payment (postage stamps, commissary, or transfer of money on the outside), they're trying to manipulate a transfer, or they think they're proving a point.

When Marion became a medium-security institution, there were several inmates who transferred to Marion that wanted to stay in SHU

and had to be cajoled into coming out onto the compound. Many arrived with fears due to the nature of their crime, past indiscretions at other prisons, or erroneous beliefs about functioning in the general population. Most of the inmates who had fears managed to overcome them once they were out of SHU. And, for the most part, they were able to remain on the compound. However, some inmates were much more challenging. These were usually the ones that had a point to prove and were more interested in being "right" than improving the quality of their life.

Within twenty-four hours of arriving at Marion, inmate Clark was in SHU. He'd torn up his mattress and thrown it onto the range. He refused to accept any property with the exception of basic clothing. He slept on the concrete floor with no mattress or blanket, by his choice. He was adamant he'd destroy any government property he was given. Clark was in prison for threatening government officials, and he continued to compose written threats and accrue more prison sentences while he was incarcerated. In terms of his demeanor in face-to-face interactions, he was a small man, articulate, and always polite, but his writings were vile. Because of his insistence on writing vicious threats to staff and government officials, he was accruing more time in SHU.

As amazing as it was, he didn't seem to mind SHU. He had calluses on his legs and ankles from sleeping on the concrete floor. Despite the cell being cold in the winter, he refused to accept a blanket. After several years of accruing longer and longer periods of SHU time for the same misconduct — with no change in behavior in sight — the decision was made to basically throw him out of SHU. And that was what happened.

He continued to compose his heinous threats, and he refused to work but received no discipline for it. There was none to give. He wanted for nothing, so nothing could be given or taken. Attempts to work with him to develop goals or rewards for good behavior also fell by the wayside, so staff allowed him to rant and rave on paper over a piece of chocolate cake that Food Service allegedly failed to put on his tray and other benign issues. Staff intercepted any mail threatening the President, judges, lawyers, et al. and Clark remained on the compound. He was a handful, to say the least.

Because of the attention from outside sources regarding the mistreatment of inmates in SHU, there was a strong push to decrease our SHU population at Marion. Thus, inmates who violated rules on a daily basis, if punished at all, weren't really punished. Case in point: There was an epidemic of contraband cell phones at the SPC.

This facility, like almost every minimum-security facility in the BOP, had no fence. Inmates were allowed a great deal of freedom in exchange for following all the rules. Cell phones are considered a serious security problem at any prison because of the nefarious plans that can be made without any ability to monitor the information. The institution telephones were monitored, obviously, but cell phones were not. The presence of these cell phones allowed inmates to schedule "drops" to be made by visitors or passersby and then picked up by inmates. As a result, access to drugs, alcohol, tobacco, and other contraband became commonplace. Prior to 2013, when minimum-security inmates were caught with cell phones, they were placed in SHU and then transferred to a low-security facility, which put them inside a fence. However, due to the recent focus on the misuse of SHU combined with a suicide by a minimum-security inmate who'd been placed in SHU at another federal facility, there was a strong push on institution staff to cease placing minimum-security inmates in SHU. At Marion, inmates were only placed in SHU if they assaulted another inmate or they literally ran from an officer who observed them engaging in misconduct.

Simultaneously, inmates in a medium-security facility were less likely to be placed in SHU. Although SHU placement may be something that's

abused at some facilities, I'm not aware of it ever being an issue where I worked. Inmates who were placed in SHU were placed there for a clear infraction or for an investigation. SHU placement was a management tool and it served a real need, its major function being to send a message that it wasn't okay to break the rules and laws. If behavior is going to change, there must be consequences.

The independent study cited above also addressed the impact of SHU on the mentally ill. Given the conclusion that restrictive housing damages inmates psychologically, there's general consensus that mentally ill inmates shouldn't be placed in SHU unless there's no other alternative. Yet, in twenty-four years of working with inmates, I can think of only one whom I believe deteriorated because of being placed in SHU, and we immediately moved him from SHU to a two-man cell in general population. His cellmate understood the inmate's special needs, and the officer imposed additional restrictions and oversight until he was stabilized.

There seems to generally be some confusion about the difference between solitary confinement and restrictive housing among those who don't work in the prison system. They aren't the same thing. In the four facilities where I worked, SHU didn't equal solitary confinement. I suspect this is true for every BOP facility except the ADX. At most

institutions, inmates in SHU are at a minimum double-celled. They're allowed at least one hour of congregate recreation per day. Multiple staff do rounds and talk to inmates every day. Some facilities, like Marion, have open grilles, so inmates can easily talk to and interact with other inmates who are housed on the same range.

That isn't to say inmates don't deteriorate in SHU, but SHU isn't the cause. They were deteriorating before they were placed in SHU. All SHU inmates are monitored closely by all staff, and they're given additional attention if there are any mental-health concerns. Inmates in SHU are more closely monitored than if they are on the compound. SHU inmates are seen by correctional staff at least twice per hour, and they're seen at least daily by psychology staff. They're checked to ensure they have no sharp objects, their sleep habits are monitored, and eating habits and hygiene are tracked. Sometimes they're celled with a mature inmate who agrees to the conditions or with another mentally ill inmate, which is sometimes therapeutic in itself. Often there's a positive response simply because of the added structure and safety features of SHU.

Sometimes inmates who are mentally ill can find the hustle and bustle of the compound overwhelming and they ask for a "time-out" in SHU. Some mentally ill inmates claim the only

time they go outside for recreation is when they're in SHU because the general population yard is too big, crowded, and threatening for them.

On occasion, SHU placement can help with medication compliance. Although inmates would not be placed in SHU simply for refusing psychotropic medication, placement in SHU following misconduct secondary to medication discontinuation sometimes served as a wake-up call. This proved to be most useful for those inmates who had some insight and declined relatively slowly, so they maintained the ability to consent to treatment.

It seems the most frequent complainers about SHU causing mental deterioration were inmates known to be highly manipulative and wanting to either be released from SHU or wanting a sedating medication so they could sleep away their SHU time.

I absolutely agree that placing someone who's actively psychotic or experiencing a major depression in solitary confinement — a place where they have no or very little human contact — can be devastating. Our restrictive housing isn't solitary confinement.

Someday, there may be funds for more mental-health facilities in the BOP or there may be an opportunity to completely revamp the correctional system into a more positive environment —

perhaps through the implementation of a token system, where inmates could earn tokens and special privileges for good behavior. But until that time, it's unfair to tie the hands of correctional officers who have such a difficult job. When an inmate is threatening you or disrespecting you in front of ten or more other inmates, you're being put in harm's way. How can it be justified to keep that inmate in the general population? There has to be an avenue to maintain control when all else fails. SHU is the failsafe.

CHAPTER 12: Gang Affiliations

For good or bad, many institutions have a strong gang influence. The Bureau attempts to identify gang members and keep rival gangs at separate institutions, but this is an arduous task. Gangs develop, change leadership, and change alliances. Inmates who have a falling out with their gang have to be separated from all the members of that gang. But finding another place for them is difficult. Sometimes the best place is at a facility that has numerous ousted gang members. But then there's the concern about the ousted gang member doing something — like assaulting a rival gang member — to make amends. Some groups are so large that it's nearly impossible to find a place to house a person who's been shunned.

There are staff members at larger institutions whose only job is to monitor gang activity on the compound. Primary concerns have to do with premeditated designated homicides ("hits"), recruitment, and large-scale disturbances. Riots evoke intense fear in both staff and inmates. Sometimes there are planned protests and sometimes things escalate spontaneously. Gang members are compelled to support their cronies, no

matter what. If one or a few have a problem, it can quickly grow. Unfortunately, the opposition is likely to also be a member of a gang, so his compatriots join in the melee. There's no real choice in the matter. Gang members have to support other members. The consequences of not supporting each other are worse than going to war for no good reason. So gang members sometimes fight even if they don't agree with the issue at hand, and sometimes they don't even know what the issue is. Gang members want to eat together and recreate in the same unit. There's strength in numbers.

Some of the most dangerous gangs, called security-threat groups, are closely monitored and tracked by the Bureau of Prisons. Gangs obviously have a negative impact on any institution. They recruit and gain influence over others through intimidation and violence. Some gangs are more savage, some more calculating. Alliances between gangs may quickly establish and then falter, sometimes without warning. Most prison gangs have a hierarchy, a purpose, or goal; they're organized or organizing (if in transition due to a change in leadership). However, in some ways, gangs, with all their violence and deconstruction, contribute order to the institution. Gangs conduct business — ranging from drugs to prostitution to laundry — and usually don't want to suffer the consequence of being "locked down," as it impacts

their shenanigans. For this reason, they attempt to resolve minor problems with the least disruption possible — at least at the older, more established penitentiaries.

In my experience, one of the most difficult groups of inmates to manage were inmates from the Washington DC area — not due to violence or disturbances but because they were so unruly. They weren't considered a gang, since there was no hierarchy, no organization, and no one seemed to have influence. In times of trouble, they'd group together, but otherwise the majority were disrespectful of one another and self-serving. They were mostly known for poor hygiene, stealing, and pimping out other inmates.

When I started at the BOP in 1989, there were a few DC inmates in the system, and they already had a reputation for being difficult. The reputation persisted for my entire career. When Washington DC's Lorton Reformatory closed in 2001, there was a huge influx of DC inmates into the federal system. Leavenworth received a few bus-loads of characters, and, true to form, they were difficult to manage. We attempted to house them with each other, but, as I mentioned before, they didn't get along with each other any better than they got along with others.

Inmate disturbances — events in which inmates, usually rivaling gangs, were in the

developing stages of a riot — were uncommon, but they did occur. Usually disturbances began on the recreation yard or in Food Service, areas where large groups of inmates gathered. These situations erupted quickly. Sometimes, if staff intervened early, before the violence, they could de-escalate the event. But sometimes they weren't successful and ended up right in the middle of it. These situations usually arose on weekends and evenings, when there were less staff on duty. All staff that were available responded, but they were always outnumbered. Lieutenants were allowed to deploy tear gas and less-than-lethal munitions. If the disturbance escalated to a point where loss of life or escape was possible, officers outside the fence (either in roving vehicles or in towers) were allowed to use deadly force to restore the orderly running of the institution.

The causes of prison violence and disturbances run the gamut, but most commonly it's an issue of perceived disrespect. This can be due to unpaid debts, encroachment, or deprecating remarks. Sometimes assaults occur to establish status within the institution or within a gang. There was a large-scale incident at Leavenworth that started over an issue in the barber shop. A large disturbance at Marion that involved approximately one hundred inmates on the recreation yard occurred over ice cream. A Hispanic inmate who

worked in Food Service had stashed some ice cream to share with his buddies. However, an arrogant black inmate found the stash and was walking around in Food Service eating it. There was a physical altercation between the two that was broken up by other inmates. Staff knew nothing about it.

There was residual tension between the two groups over this incident. In an attempt to resolve it, the shot-callers for the black and Hispanic groups were to meet on the recreation yard to discuss concessions for the disrespect and ice cream. The meeting was expected to be civil. The Hispanics were on the recreation yard first. Suddenly, a large group of black inmates exited the building heading for the yard. The Hispanics concluded these men were arriving en masse to fight. So they (the Hispanics) made a preemptive strike. There were rocks and loose concrete on the yard as a result of some recent construction. The Hispanics made use of this material and began hurling it toward the black inmates. A large disturbance ensued.

What actually happened was a softball game that was frequented by many black inmates was scheduled for that night. The black inmates weren't there to fight; they were there to watch a game.

The unpredictability of inmate behavior is just another aspect of the challenge of working in this environment. At Leavenworth, while I was standing in a hallway with several inmates who were entering and leaving the department, I saw a frail, older, mentally ill, white inmate point his finger at a large black inmate and say, "Fuck you, nigger." My eyes about fell out of my head. There was no doubt in anyone's mind, except the black inmate's, that there were going to be serious repercussions. No one could have predicted it would matter that the white inmate was mentally ill; but it did matter to the black inmate. He let the whole thing slide.

CHAPTER 13: Jackers

They're called "jackers" or "gunslingers" (gunners), the inmates who repeatedly expose their genitals or come up with creative ways to masturbate in the presence of staff — primarily the female staff. In general, this type of misconduct is rare at lower-security institutions. I'd been warned about it before I started at USP Leavenworth. I expected it, although I don't know how I expected it to occur, as I really hadn't given it much thought.

I was in a group room, facilitating a drug education group of about twenty inmates. I could see into the hallway through the windows of the group room, which lined the wall to my right. There was an inmate in the hallway who was standing at the outer edge of my field of vision looking at me, but not staring. I was focused on the group members and busy teaching something profound about drug treatment when I noticed the inmate moving ever so slightly into and out of my vision. He was holding a broom, as if he might be an orderly. As he moved in and out of my vision, leaning just slightly one way and then the other, I started to wonder if he was holding something in his hand other than the broomstick. No, couldn't

be! He was standing in a hallway. He didn't look like my idea of a pervert — no overcoat, not disheveled, not creepy, not large and intimidating. He was just an average, young black man. So I continued to try to focus on my group.

In retrospect, I can imagine what he must have concluded, given that he knew I'd seen him and did nothing. After several more minutes of me observing this behavior, I finally came to accept that what I was seeing was, in fact, what I suspected — an inmate standing in the hallway with his penis in his hand and stroking it while I was facilitating this group. So I excused myself from the group and walked into the hallway. I asked a fantastic question, "What are you doing?" in a tone more accusatory than inquisitive. He didn't answer, but when I asked him his name, he said, "Johnson." His name wasn't Johnson. I didn't get the humor until later.

Not too long after that, there was an inmate in one of my groups who surprised me with his antics but turned out to be a typical jacker, as my later experience would teach me. He was black, engaging, and friendly. He was a good participant in group, quickly grasping concepts and contributing relevant experiences. One day, I was showing a drug-education video. The inmate was sitting in the front row. I was standing in the open doorway watching the video as the inmates sat in

the moderately darkened room. When I gazed around the room, there he was, staring at me and busy with his exposed penis, jacking away. I have no idea if those sitting around him were complicit or if they were unaware. I hear that "back in the day," behavior of this nature would never have been tolerated by other inmates. Well, on that day, it was.

Despite other inmates' stated disgust for inmates who disrespect staff in this manner, I don't know of any inmate who's been assaulted for jacking. That doesn't mean it hasn't happened, but it doesn't happen a lot. In open penitentiaries, inmates have a system for masturbating while watching staff members. "Jiggers" (inmates who stand watch for and warn other inmates when staff are coming) are used while others masturbate and then they switch off. Almost like a small gang.

The most extreme jackers (those who have more than ten prison sanctions for this type of behavior) tend to have a similar disposition. They often are very demanding and have poor impulse control. Both male and female staff members find these inmates exhausting. For these inmates, public masturbation seems to be just one more symptom in a long line of symptoms associated with a severe personality disorder, usually marked by issues of entitlement, emotional lability, problems with taking responsibility, and an inability to delay

gratification. When they want something, they want it immediately and become overly upset when their demands aren't met.

Marion had some of the most willful self-stimulators. They were more extreme, some having thirty or more incident reports for inappropriate sexual behavior during their incarceration. Seemingly, nothing deterred them. And, for several of them, they weren't selective. Male staff had a particularly difficult time with these inmates when they were the target of this behavior.

One inmate in particular seemed to only target male staff. Because of bravado, many of the staff didn't want to acknowledge it and certainly didn't want to write incident reports for this type of infraction. Once a few male staff wrote reports, it quickly became apparent he was victimizing many more male staff than anyone wanted to admit.

This particular inmate had been at Leavenworth when I was there but I didn't really have much contact with him. When he transferred to Marion, he'd accumulated years of SHU time on his record. The executive staff thought it might be beneficial to let him have a new start, clear the record, and put him in general population. The inmate didn't appreciate his reprieve and only lasted a few weeks before breaking the rules and going to SHU. His modus operandi was to make threats, smear feces all over his cell, and masturbate to staff. He was

considered quite disgusting by most staff, who sometimes called him "mud-dauber." However, with me, he was polite, respectful, and seemed intelligent. He enjoyed having lofty discussions about racial issues, philosophical debates about the meaning of good and bad, etc.

This inconsistent behavior with different staff was not uncommon with inmates. Those outside the system seem to find this difficult to fully comprehend. Inmates can be very charming when they choose to be, making it difficult for an observer to believe they could engage in outrageous behavior.

This inmate often warranted a calculated-use-of-force team to move him from one cell to another, usually because he'd smeared so much fecal material that the stench was unbearable, not to mention unsanitary. He'd refuse to move, so a team would suit up, but he'd always submit prior to any struggle. It wasn't until I witnessed the full procedure that it finally dawned on me what was going on. It was actually quite obvious. When a team "suits up," five staff, almost always buff men, put on black garb with pads and helmets. When an inmate submits to restraints immediately, before the team rushes in on him and forces him into restraints, he's calmly placed in handcuffs behind his back and encircled by these five large men. He's then stripped of all his clothing, placed in new

clothing, and moved to another cell. For a small, homosexual male, this has to be very exciting.

B. Forrest received over 120 incident reports in seventeen years, sixty-eight of them for either masturbating or indecent exposure. Forrest was indiscriminant, victimizing both female and male staff. Although all inmates who engaged in this type of behavior were repulsive, he was particularly offensive, probably because he was so brazen. He'd stand in his cell completely naked, fondling a nipple and stroking his penis while staff made rounds. He'd stick his penis out of the food slot when meals were being delivered. He refused to control his behavior. Most inmates would be respectful for short periods of time or to certain staff if they wanted something. Forrest was consistently and universally repugnant.

As evidence of his perversion, he attempted to sexually assault a civilian while incarcerated. He alleged he'd been physically abused by several correctional officers after they intervened to stop his assault on another inmate. Forrest filed a lawsuit against the officers, which gave him the opportunity for a legal deposition to be taken. Forrest was in full restraints — handcuffed in the front with cuffs secured to a belly chain and in leg restraints. He was escorted to the front office where an attorney and female court reporter interviewed him. Two officers were present. While seated, he

was somehow able to remove his penis from his pants and, in one move, leap onto the table, land on his knees and lunge at the court reporter with his erect penis. Before he was able to make contact with her, the officers intervened and gained control of the situation. Soon after, Forrest decided to drop his lawsuit. It's worth mentioning that there was no record of him engaging in this type of behavior prior to or following his incarceration.

There had been a variety of interventions made at Marion to gain control over the constant barrage of exposed erect penises. These included increasing normal sanctions (SHU time or loss of commissary or telephone privileges, etc.), attempting to extinguish the behavior by ignoring it, having inmates watch videos instructing them on appropriate behavior (including females telling them what they really think about it), and reinforcing good behavior with more staff interaction. I know that at other facilities inmates were required to wear jumpsuits with no pockets when they were out of their cells to decrease access. Some facilities have also attempted to have inmates wear special emblems or clothing to alert others to the types of behavior that might be displayed. This last idea was probably the best, but it was shot down due to concerns about lawsuits. The inmates complained, ironically, that the BOP

was exposing them as exposers and therefore putting them at risk.

One day when I was at USP Leavenworth, an inmate was masturbating as I walked by his cell and it really pissed me off, as it always did. I stopped and walked back to his cell in D-cell house, one of the SHU overflow units. My goal was to look at the cell number so I could get his name and write an incident report. This unit hadn't been renovated and had open grilles, not doors, with a small catwalk down each range. Just as I got back to his cell, he ejaculated and it went all over my sweater. I was on the fifth tier about halfway down the range. All I could think about was getting out of that sweater. I had to walk down the rest of the tier, passing several inmates, wait for an officer to open the tier door, descend five stories, and get to the officers' station. Somehow, I did it. And, no, the sweater was never worn again. When I transferred to Marion a year later, that inmate was there. It was difficult to not have extreme animosity toward him.

That wasn't my only clothing casualty. At Marion, I was contacted to help with another use-of-force team. The warden had been assaulted, and the inmate, N. Esparza, needed to be moved. While the warden and associate warden were walking through SHU, an inmate threw feces on the warden. It was rare for a warden to be assaulted.

The inmate had been placed in SHU for a couple of weeks earlier, after throwing feces at a female correctional officer.

So, here was the setting: I was there to talk to an inmate who was in a cell with an open grille and who'd just thrown feces at the warden and had a recent history of sliming a female officer. I'd never had any problems with Esparza. He was normally quiet and respectful when interacting with me, but today could be different. I was wearing a new jacket; it was the first time I'd worn it, but that wasn't on my mind at the time. My greatest concern was that I might soon be wearing the inmate's feces on my face.

I approached the cell followed by a lieutenant, a person with a video camera, and five officers dressed for combat. I wasn't interested in standing too close to the inmate, so I created as much distance as I could, which put me about eight feet away with my back pressed against the recreation cage grille. Esparza was calm and cooperative. He immediately agreed to be restrained and was escorted to a closed-front cell on another range. As I walked off the range, an officer brought my attention to the feces on the back of my jacket. The feces that hadn't hit the warden had landed on the wall and grille across the corridor — the one I'd leaned against when I was talking to the inmate.

Now it was on my jacket. My jacket went into the SHU trash can.

Having several inmates masturbate as they interact with you, experiencing shock at what you see when you instruct a class, or becoming aware of what's going on underneath the table while you are tasked with overseeing inmates eating lunch can change a person. I developed a new practice of taking in a wider visual picture than I ever had before, both inside and outside of prison. In general, I used to only look at a man's face. If I took in the whole person, it was usually only at a distance, such as when I was walking in a mall or sitting in a lecture hall. Within a very short time, I changed into a person who was visually aware of the total person before me at all times. If an inmate was in my office and sitting too close to my desk, I asked him to put his hands where I could see them. And I don't mind telling you that when I'm in the community, I'm now aware — hypervigilant even — of a stranger's crotch to ensure nothing is exposed or being massaged. This is only one of the many ways prison has affected my personal life.

Professionally, my clothing style changed. During the last eleven years of my career, I wore baggy pants and a large windbreaker, every day, all day, regardless of the weather, including those days when it was over a hundred degrees. There

were several female staff members at Marion who ended up adopting this fashion trend.

CHAPTER 14: The Men of G Unit

Ultimately, the administration at Marion decided to move the most well-known and unyielding masturbators at Marion to one unit, G-Lower. G Unit had solid doors with a little window at the top of the door to see into the cell and for air circulation, and a food slot at the middle of the door. There were eighteen cells on one side and sixteen cells on the other. The cells faced each other across a narrow corridor. The officers' station was at the front of the unit, separated from the cells by an additional grille. Female staff didn't go onto the range unless it was unavoidable. The inmates hated it. They hated the absence of women and they hated the unit. The unit was dirtier, darker, and dingier than the others. They'd remain there for at least six months and mustn't engage in any misconduct. There were a few that seemed to get the message. When they were moved from G Unit, they didn't return. But then, there were others.

On one occasion, I needed to tell an inmate in G-Lower that his young son was dead. Usually this was handled by one of the chaplains, but none were available. While I was talking to the inmate at the front of the range, separated by a locked grille,

another inmate stood behind him acting like he was using the sink in the mop closet. There was no doubt he knew the content of the conversation, but he took the opportunity to masturbate while watching our interaction. I knew the inmate who lost his son from Leavenworth. He'd disrespected me a few times, but I still felt bad for him. The inmate who stood behind him was one of those guys who usually presented as social, friendly, and polite — just one more example of a person who pretended to have a soul.

It didn't take long for some of the inmates banished to G Unit to figure out that if they fought with one another, they couldn't continue to be housed together on the same range. This behavior would usually necessitate a move to SHU, which had open grilles and female staff walking ranges at least once per week.

Two well-known inmates (and by that I mean difficult) who were housed on G Unit went at each other during a congregate recreation period. A black inmate, who came by his placement on G Unit deservedly, pulled a knife (shank) on a Middle-Eastern Muslim inmate. The Muslim inmate was in G Unit because there was nowhere else to place him. He'd exhausted all other options. The potential victim took the weapon away and used it on his assailant, stabbing him in the left cheek. The wounded black inmate was taken to the

local hospital. In addition to being loud and belligerent, he refused medical treatment. I was asked to meet with the inmate and convince him to comply. When I arrived at the emergency room, I found the inmate with a gaping hole in his face, cussing and yelling, hair in two high pigtails, sitting up in bed like a child having a tantrum. He was cuffed to the bed and the two officers guarding him looked nonplussed. After a great deal of time, energy, and attempts to reason with him, he agreed to treatment. He was eventually transferred to the ADX. He'd outstayed his welcome at Marion.

There were other strategies for getting out of G Unit. One of the least mature and most demanding inmates who'd been living on one of the lower ranges in G Unit and found his way to SHU took the opportunity to force frequent contact with staff. His usual approach was to complain he was suicidal.

The BOP requires all potentially suicidal inmates to be assessed by psychology staff. At that time, it wasn't dictated that it must be done every single time an inmate made a threat, but we generally responded unless there were multiple threats within the same day and/or clear game playing was afoot. There were some weeks I was called to SHU every day to meet with this inmate. I remember on one occasion being called to SHU to talk with him and finding him naked and

masturbating in his cell. When I walked away, he yelled down the range, "I'm going to kill myself," and my response was, "Good luck with that." No, not professional, but sometimes enough is enough. He never did hurt himself.

Regarding the BOP's policy on suicide assessments, the inmate gets to decide when they need to be assessed for suicide just by uttering the words. The idea that someone other than a psychologist — someone familiar with the inmate and the situation — could determine if the inmate needed to be assessed for suicide was shunned. On the surface, this made sense. Correctional officers, lieutenants, and unit managers aren't trained in this area. However, there were often occasions when assessment just wasn't necessary and it didn't take someone with expertise to determine this.

When I transferred to Marion, the Chief Psychologist at the time was called out to the institution frequently after hours. Keep in mind there were only 400 inmates at that time. It was readily apparent the inmates were finding this extra attention reinforcing, which was increasing the reported incidences of suicidal ideation.

When I was the Chief Psychologist, I worked with the lieutenants, so they'd talk with the inmate before notifying a psychologist after hours. Inmates were stating they were suicidal when they couldn't

get a cell change or their commissary wasn't delivered on time or they wanted a book. When this was the situation, the inmate was told it would be addressed in the morning. And it always was. The result was a dramatic decrease in reported suicidal ideation. Immediately responding every time — which was expected by the BOP — was only serving to reinforce manipulative and impulsive behavior.

The pinnacle of my "enough is enough" was an inmate who required excessive attention and repeatedly requested services, including psychiatric services. He was taking an antidepressant medication, an SSRI. When an inmate needed medication or a medication change, he'd be brought to a special room above Health Services where he'd interact with a psychiatrist via satellite. The staff psychologist was responsible for setting up the scheduled appointment and was present to share information and ensure accurate information was provided.

This particular inmate often complained of side effects from his medication and frequently requested to be seen by the psychiatrist. As I had responsibility over telepsychiatry at the time, I was the frequent victim of his habit of appearing for the session with his penis exposed out of his crotch-ripped clothing when meeting with the psychiatrist. There were no repercussions for his behavior. He couldn't be denied services. Denying

services was a sure way to cause problems for me and the BOP. He was nearly always in SHU, and he had numerous incident reports for his behavior, which had no impact. I could have terminated that session but then I'd have to do it all over again the following month.

On one particular day, this inmate was out in the unit recreation yard and refused to return to his cell. I was requested to assist in convincing him to comply. The inmate was inside the fenced yard and I was outside the fence. When I arrived, the inmate was already full of venom. Before I knew it, we were both yelling at each other. I don't make a habit of yelling at inmates. Then he spit on me. So I spit back. I'm not a good spitter — poor aim, no distance. But I was fuming. I had a strong desire to beat that inmate silly. Of course, I didn't, and eventually I was pulled away by another staff member.

In regard to the concern that some of these inmates may be mentally ill and not able to control their behavior, this is certainly possible. That doesn't change the fact that staff have to deal with it, either way.

Research suggests there's potential benefit in using high doses of antidepressants or administering female hormones to reduce male sex drive. But, as in the community, medication can only be issued with consent unless the individual is

deemed by a court of law to be a danger to himself or others, and that certainly wasn't the case here. As stated previously, these inmates have difficulty taking responsibility for their behavior, making it almost impossible to enlist their genuine interest in treatment. In addition, using medication in this fashion straddles the fence between medicating for behavior control and treating a primary mental illness — a gray area that makes most professionals uncomfortable.

I'm aware of only one federal inmate who was authorized to receive Depo-Provera to reduce sex-offending behavior. Depo injections are usually used by women as a long-acting, reversible, hormonal contraceptive. This drug has controversially been called "chemical castration" when used with male sex offenders. The Bureau of Prisons would rarely sanction its use.

This inmate had been determined to be sexually dangerous, civilly committed, and detained in a special facility in Butner, North Carolina. That meant he was in a hospital setting where he was afforded the opportunity to participate in treatment. Most inmates committed under the Adam Walsh Child Protection and Safety Act of 2006 didn't participate and instead spent their time arguing about the legality of their situation.

During this inmate's civil commitment, he threatened a judge. It's suspected this was

contrived, with the goal of receiving a new sentence, getting transferred out of the civil commitment unit, and returning to the familiar comfort of a correctional facility. Because he'd been authorized to receive Depo prior to the transfer, we were allowed to maintain him on the medication.

Overall, throughout the federal prison system, the vast majority of inmates don't publicly masturbate. They don't expose their genitals to staff. They don't cut holes in their pockets or pants or attach things to their genitals so they're stimulated when they move.

In response to the question, "What do you expect when these men are deprived of relations with females?" the answer is, I expect the norm. I expect inmates to act like human beings, or at the very least, like most inmates. Ask yourself: If you were in prison, would you expose yourself to staff over and over again despite the adverse effects this behavior has on your privileges?

A few years after the mission change (which I describe at length in Chapter 16) when Marion became a medium-security facility, someone from the central office called and wanted a list of those inmates that had been housed in G Unit as a result of chronic, inappropriate sexual behavior. I couldn't locate a roster, so I was asked to send a list of everyone we could remember. I obliged without asking the purpose of the inquiry. Several months

later, it became clear. The named inmates were tracked in their current institutions to see if they were continuing to engage in this behavior. They were. Therefore, it was concluded that isolating these inmates from female staff wasn't an effective deterrent and shouldn't continue.

Here was the big problem with this decision: It came about based on my memory. Who do I remember most? The inmates who were on G Unit for the longest time, the ones that were chronically in need of attention, and the ones with the biggest behavioral problems. I don't remember the ones who were on the unit for the minimum amount of time and moved out without another incident.

CHAPTER 15: From Supermaxed to Oversexed

On Wednesday June 28, 2006, there was an announcement to staff that United Stated Penitentiary Marion would be changing to a Federal Correctional Institution, going from a supermax to a medium-security facility. We were told the reason for the change was due to budget constraints. I believe the Bureau of Prisons thought they could assimilate most of the Marion inmates into open penitentiaries, which were less costly to operate. They were wrong.

The vast majority of Marion staff hadn't worked at a mainline facility, a facility where inmates walked among staff without being in shackles. There was concern about how well staff would respond to this change. They were used to working in a locked-down, supermax facility. It had been this way for twenty-four years.

In March 2007, our mission changed and we became a medium-security, sex-offender-management-program facility. Marion as a supermax had some of the most despicable characters — inmates who'd kidnapped and tortured, inmates who'd killed their children or raped and killed other people's children — but most were just run-of-the-

mill murderers, drug dealers, and organized-crime types who couldn't be managed at other institutions.

After the mission change, approximately half of Marion's inmate population had a past arrest or conviction for a sex offense. I'm not sure who was involved in the decision to change Marion's mission, but I'm sure it wasn't anyone who worked at Marion. We knew Marion served an important function and that many of the supermax inmates wouldn't fare well anywhere else.

Marion had managed a unique population, and it was no surprise to us that within a few years of transferring our original population to other high-level facilities, there was an urgency to change two existing prisons into "Special Management Unit" facilities, which basically sounded like modified supermax facilities. It's also worth noting that several of Marion's previous inmates were involved in violent behavior after their transfers, which resulted in either them being killed or killing others.

For some inmates, Marion supermax had been a haven. Inmates who didn't function well anywhere else felt safe because they were separated from nearly everyone else. If they chose to come out of their single-man cell for the two hours of recreation each day, they only had to deal with seventeen other inmates, at most. They had a personal

television they could watch without worrying about someone changing the channel or where to sit in a large television room. Their meals were brought to the unit and served in their cell, thus they didn't have to go to a large dining hall, stand in line, and sit with others to eat. For some, every moment with other inmates was frightening because they were constantly worried about being assaulted. Their history may involve hurting a child, cooperating with the government, or assaulting/murdering a gang member. There was fear of retaliation. For some inmates, the structure of a locked-down facility added to a sense of security. Daily routines were less susceptible to change when you were locked in a cell most of the day. There were fewer degrees of freedom and things were more predictable.

Several inmates who were transferred to Marion supermax from state facilities expressed appreciation for the professionalism of the staff. Occasionally, state facilities contract with the federal prison system and vice versa. If either system has difficulty managing an inmate or if the inmate has too many separatees, the other system is used — for a fee, of course. Inmates who'd been incorrigible at other institutions often adapted quickly and complied with all expectations after transferring to Marion. When it came to transferring out due to the mission change, several

inmates expressed a great deal of concern and didn't want to leave. To help these inmates with the transition, staff at receiving facilities were contacted and informed about the inmate's proclivities and mental health needs. Many of those who had concerns did relatively well. One inmate who transferred from a Washington State facility with a long dossier of assaults on staff and inmates as well as destruction of property didn't have one incident of this type while at Marion. He eventually ended up at a medium-security facility and did well.

Mission changes are always a large undertaking, and it was no different for Marion. Although Marion had around 385 inmates when I arrived, after building and activating four new units in 2004, the population had grown to 530. This was still small compared to all other facilities. However, most of these inmates had several separations from inmates within the facility and inmates at other facilities. Therefore, a great deal of time was spent strategizing how and where to transfer these inmates. Roster after roster was reviewed to ensure inmates' safety. Given the number of inmates who had separations at our facility and the enormous amount of inmates who had separations at other facilities, all moves were checked and double checked.

A "bus crew" of staff was tasked with driving the busloads of inmates to United States Penitentiaries located in Coleman, Florida; Beaumont, Texas; Terre Haute, Indiana; Florence, Colorado; Atlanta, Georgia; Lewisburg, Pennsylvania, and elsewhere. Safety and security were a large concern. As a bus moved down the highway, escape was much more likely than when an inmate was behind a wall. In addition, many of these inmates had nothing to lose. A third of them had no release date, meaning they were sentenced to life or they had fifty-year sentences. Many were considered particularly dangerous because they had resources in the community. Despite this, all inmates were safely delivered to their destinations.

The institution was slowly emptied out. Some inmates were placed on buses immediately and others were moved around the institution so that those going to specific institutions were placed together to await the next bus. Of all the inmates who transferred from the USP during the mission change, only one bucked and had to be forced to go. He was placed on a gurney, in restraints, with a camera on him. The camera was used whenever possible to circumvent any potential lawsuits. He was then placed in a van that followed the bus to his new institution. It was always better, if possible, to keep disruptive inmates away from compliant inmates, especially on long transports.

Certainly all Bureau of Prisons correctional staff have heard the words, "Attention all radio units…," usually followed by information about some emergency situation. At Marion, this message was accompanied by the sound of alarms in the background that were occurring simultaneously in the control center. Those words and that alert sound caused immediate response. But, on Thursday September 14, 2006, at 10:20 a.m., I heard, "Attention all radio units (a brief pause), the inside count is now zero." The last three to leave were inmates Knorr, Sahakian, and McIntosh, members of the Aryan Brotherhood who'd been held in special cells for several years awaiting their re-trial (following a mistrial) for the murder of a black DC inmate in 1999.

When we left the prison that day, all the grilles were open. Previously, one grille would be opened at a time and closed after you walked through. If you weren't in good favor with the control room officer, movement through the institution could take a very long time. Being able to just walk freely through the building was beyond strange.

The institution would remain empty for six months. During that time, everything was painted, floors were retiled, walls were torn down, walls were built, and the visiting room was redone to allow for contact visits. The dining area was expanded, the commissary was rebuilt, beds were

added to the new unit cells, the electronic control centers for the new units were relocated, and the facilities department was updated to allow for inmate crews. The towers were decommissioned, rows of razor-wire fences were removed, the message center (which had been an added measure of security) was decommissioned, and the main control center was redone.

In addition, staff were retrained. The vast majority of staff had never worked at an open facility or with medium-security inmates. To assist with this, all staff who hadn't worked at an open facility in the past five years were bussed, for four consecutive days, to and from the closest federal prison, FCI Greenville, Illinois, to spend the day among inmates. Although many staff complained about the bus ride, I believe the experience was helpful for most of them.

After six months, we started receiving inmates. We were extremely fortunate to have the down time between the maximum- and medium-security inmates. Our transition was gradual, orderly, and palatable. This was in contrast to USP Leavenworth, which transitioned from a high-security to a medium-security facility soon after we did. Their transition was much less pleasant, out of necessity. Because of Hurricane Rita, which destroyed large sections of the FCI Beaumont

complex in Beaumont, Texas, their mission change occurred within one week.

To increase the chances of successfully transitioning to a sex-offender facility, one in which sex offenders felt comfortable on the compound, we had to achieve "critical mass." This was an arbitrarily picked number (forty-five percent) of how many sex-offending inmates needed to be on the compound to ensure sex offenders would remain on the compound. The idea was to create a situation where there were too many sex offenders for other inmates to scare into requesting protective custody and checking into SHU. At most facilities, there were a small percentage of sex-offenders. It was easy to intimidate and victimize them. If nearly half of the population was sex offenders, they would feel less threatened. To ease the process, the decision was made to balance the number of incoming inmates from the beginning, ensuring the types of inmates arriving on buses alternated between sex offenders and non-sex offenders. Our first busload held forty-five sex-offending inmates, the second had forty-five non-sex offending inmates, etc. Our bus crew made runs one or two times per week until the institution was full. The group of arriving inmates was, as expected, much more pleasant than the inmates we'd shipped six months prior. One of the officers who was part of the regular bus crew stated he

nearly wrecked the bus when he sneezed and one of the new inmates said, "Bless you."

Everything went pretty well with our plan except for the chow hall seating. Inmates were called to eat either by their housing unit or their work site. Inmates came in, took a tray, were served food by inmates in a cafeteria style, and sat wherever they wanted in the room. Inmates self-segregate. In our case, all the Native Americans sat at the tables on the left side of the dining hall and the blacks all sat at the tables on the far right side of the dining hall. The center section developed into the most problematic area. Initially, there was a relatively large Latino population and they sat in the center rows, closest to the dish tank. The white inmates sat at the center rows closest to the serving line.

From the beginning, the white inmates further segregated between sex offenders and non-sex offenders. White non-sex offenders were much less tolerant of sex offenders than were the other groups. They'd do research to determine who was who and enforce seating rules. It turned out that the white sex offenders, who were nestled in a small section between the Hispanic tables and the white non-sex-offender tables, didn't have adequate seating. Although they were the largest group, they wouldn't assert themselves. They'd stand holding their food trays and wait for a seat

in "their section," despite the fact there were empty tables in the rows right next to them. This continued even after a significant number of Latino inmates were placed in SHU and ultimately transferred to other institutions due to a large disturbance on the recreation yard. The Latinos held onto their real estate even though there was clearly no need for it.

There were several attempts by staff to intervene, but drastic changes can cause a serious disturbance. Having an officer assign inmates to specific seats as they went through the serving line or to fill up tables in one row before going to the next was considered a bad idea. These were the times that discussions about "Who's running this institution?" occurred. There was a great deal of value in understanding how to pick our battles. Making decisions that cause the inmate population to unite against staff can be catastrophic.

One warden attempted to redistribute inmate workers so there was more balance in job assignments; i.e., there tended to be a large sex-offender population that worked in the Education Department, so when they were called to eat, those tables filled up faster. Several of the sex offenders were outraged that staff didn't "rescue" them and complained about our insensitivity to their issue. Some of the sex offenders also complained that staff didn't intervene to help them on the unit when

inmates wouldn't allow them to sit in certain sections to watch television.

Wardens added as many tables as could fit to the dining area. But inmates were all about equal distribution, so although the blacks, Native Americans, and Hispanics didn't need more tables, if the white inmates got a table, an additional table must be provided to the others. Otherwise, we'd be accused of discriminating.

Staff weren't necessarily insensitive but they weren't familiar with inmates who were unwilling to stand up for themselves, nor were staff willing to condone this type of behavior, which was seen as manipulative. So inmates continued to stand at mainline if the tables self-designated as sex-offender tables were full. This occurred for years. To my knowledge, there was never a resolution. When inmates complained during meal time, staff would tell them to sit at any empty table. They never complied.

There were also some hiccups with the layout of the facility. The hallways were built for a population of 500 not 1,000. So the hallways were very crowded during inmate moves. Eventually, staff decided to divide the moves so there'd be fewer inmates in the hallways at one time.

Another issue was the absence of air conditioning in the dining area. When Marion was a supermax, camp inmates would come into the

kitchen area, prepare the meals, and clean up afterward. There were only fifty inmates who ate their meals in Food Service. Staff would stand for about twenty minutes to monitor the dining area while the inmates ate, so the absence of air conditioning in the dining area was tolerable.

With the mission change, it was no longer necessary to have camp inmates prepare meals because the medium-security inmates worked in the kitchen. The dining area and kitchen were made larger, and a dish room was added at the front of the dining area to accommodate their needs. The amount of time standing "mainline" increased to around ninety minutes. With the added heat from the kitchen, dish room, and additional bodies, the discomfort also increased. In the summer, it could be more than a hundred degrees in the dining area. Sweat running down your back and pooling at your tail bone while you're wearing your business casuals wasn't pleasant. Some staff brought handheld fans. Oftentimes, wardens allowed department heads to forgo wearing neckties when the weather was extreme.

Soon after the mission change, it was so hot and humid in the inmate dining room that water dripped off the ceiling like a tropical rain falling onto the tables, chairs, inmates and their food as they ate. This was apparently caused by the dish tank's contribution to the humidity. A ventilation

system was installed after a few weeks, which helped with the need for an umbrella. Inmates complained about the heat but seemed to appreciate that they were there for only fifteen minutes, whereas we had to stand for the duration. Finally, after a few years, a warden got approval to air condition the Food Service area. The BOP bought three Big Ass Fans (this was the name of the product), and the facilities department installed a cooling system. This change greatly improved my work day.

CHAPTER 16: Sex Offenders: Any Age, Any Sex

Working with sex offenders presented some unique challenges. Staff were supposed to be unbiased, but it was difficult with this population. There was a general dislike by both inmates and staff of those who sexually abused children. Staff were encouraged to not read the details of an inmate's case unless it was necessary. There was a natural tendency when reading an inmate's case history to replace the image of the victim with a child you knew, making it even more distasteful.

Some staff didn't need to know the details of an inmate's story to feel disdain for him. There were complaints by inmates that certain job supervisors wouldn't hire sex offenders, certain units wouldn't give sex offenders the good cells (in front of the television), or certain staff would call them derogatory names. The most common name was "cho-mo," a contraction for child molester. Despite this, I think most staff did a pretty good job of keeping their prejudices in check, overall.

It's true that sex offenders are the most disliked group among inmates, and they generally aren't able to remain on the compound at the vast majority of institutions. Historically, inmates

might be able to keep their offenses hidden and function adequately for a period of time, but now, with technology, it's easy for inmates to find anyone's background. At most institutions, sex offenders are assaulted or told to "check-in" (meaning, go to the Special Housing Unit and never come out) before they're assaulted.

Many of the sex offenders at Marion who did any time at other institutions appreciated that they were able to remain on the compound. They knew what it was like to have to do time in protective custody, where they didn't have access to programming. However, the inmates with convictions for sex offending who were new to the system didn't seem to understand how lucky they were to be at a facility that was created so they could remain in general population. They tended to focus on the inadequacies. Many of their complaints were similar to those of any inmate who was perceived as weak, such as being intimidated into certain seating in the chow hall or in the unit. Although these were valid concerns, it was difficult to get past their demands to be rescued by staff as opposed to attempting to resolve their own issues.

All sex offenders are not created equal. There are those who rape adults, those that prefer teenagers, those who target children, and some who victimize toddlers and even infants. Some prefer males, some females, and some have no

preference. Some are sadistic and enjoy hurting others; some engage in the behavior only once, supposedly; some repeatedly target the same victim; some had many victims; and some prefer their own children. Some sex offenders who victimize children don't necessarily prefer children. They're antisocial, want sex, and the most available subject happens to be the child seated near them. Not all child sex offenders are pedophiles or individuals that sustain a sexual desire for children over a period of time.

Some are unable/unwilling to consider the harmfulness of their offense, claiming they're only expressing their love to the victim and adamantly denying they cause any kind of harm or trauma. Some rationalize their behavior by stating she/he wanted it, or they were intoxicated at the time, or they were conducting sex education, or they were doing research and their goal was to be helpful. Others claim it was a compulsion, a behavior they detest but cannot control. Some of those who molest children engage in this behavior because their social skills are so poor they can't relate to adults and claim to feel comfortable only with children. And there are those who are convicted for sex with a teen and seem sincere when maintaining they didn't know his/her age, but these are few and far between.

One of the memorable explanations was a reportedly religious individual who claimed it was a sin to have sex outside of his marriage. So he had sex with his prepubescent daughters. Since they were an extension of his wife, he reasoned that it wasn't a sin.

Research into the etiology, course, and treatment of sex offenders was a relatively new area of study in the world of psychology and corrections during my tenure. There were many different theories of the causes and treatment, and there continues to be a growing interest/need in this area.

At Marion, sex offenders were offered and encouraged to participate in treatment. Those that were considered high risk for reoffending and were within a few years of release had the opportunity to participate in a residential treatment program (living in one unit together). Those that were considered low to moderate risk could participate in a non-residential program (they were dispersed throughout the facility and attended groups for several hours per week). Motivation for participation varied. Several inmates who'd been sentenced prior to the late 1980s and were eligible for parole participated. The possibility of parole was a great motivator.

The vast majority of Marion's sex offenders were convicted for crimes that involved actual contact

with their victims (as opposed to internet contact or possession of child pornography), and this was generally accomplished by "grooming" the victim. Most of these predators didn't physically force themselves on their targets. Instead, they slowly and methodically enticed the victim into agreeing to some type of sexual contact and then got them to agree to keep the secret through promises, intimidation, or threats. Although you might imagine there is a "type" of person that would do this, there is not.

Some presented as confident, articulate, intelligent, and had wives or adult partners. Some were socially awkward and insecure, even self-deprecating. Some were obsequious, manipulative, and slimy. There were business professionals, lawyers, mayors, doctors, and teachers. Some were young, appeared youthful, attractive, and innocent; some were older and unattractive. The commonality was they were universally able to manipulate and con children or others who were naïve, including trusting adults. It happens. No shame there. Most people want to believe that others — especially relatives, friends, and teachers — are good people. However, what's amazing and disheartening is how many victims and victim's families continue to trust these guys even after they've been convicted.

Most inmates are manipulative; it seems to be one of the main characteristics of being a criminal. Staff-monitored phone calls revealed the constant lies and half-truths being told by inmates about why they were placed in SHU, the abuse they received, how much they loved their wives/multiple partners ("Could you send money?"), how they were being threatened or extorted ("Could you send money?"), and, more often than you might think, that they couldn't take it anymore or were going to kill themselves ("Could you send money?").

The most disconcerting, though, are the conversations with loved ones or friends of those that were sexually victimized. The degree of manipulation is remarkable, mostly because it's so obvious to those not involved. Often there are religious/repentant overtones intermixed with elicited guilt in the recipient. Sometimes there's a payoff in the form of wives/mothers/victims wanting to visit. Mind boggling.

There was quite a balancing act that was required by staff to protect the public while not violating the inmate's civil liberties. If staff became aware of an attempt to have a minor victim visit, the visit was denied. Staff weren't always aware, though. Children don't have identification cards. If the accompanying adult, perhaps a mom or sister, identifies the child as someone other than the victim, staff have no way of knowing. And often, to

protect anonymity, the child's name is not listed in the pre-sentence investigation report, which is the paperwork available to staff regarding the inmate's offense and personal background.

M. Green called his family every day and ended every sickeningly sweet conversation with prayer, usually around the theme of forgiveness. His wife wanted to bring his sixteen-year-old daughter, whom Green had victimized, to visit. The daughter wrote letters to the administration asking for permission. Green had a long sentence. He wasn't participating in treatment. In fact, he was currently housed, at his request, with a young, awkward inmate. He'd indicated that he'd look after the young man. Staff suspected he was grooming this inmate, but the young inmate repeatedly denied this to several staff. When older inmates asked to house with younger inmates, it was a red flag; but if both inmates indicated it was their preference and there was no indication of impropriety, it was allowed.

Regardless of Green's behavior in the institution, the daughter's request was considered and denied because she was a minor. Two years later, when she was eighteen, she requested again. Although staff weren't at all comfortable with it, the decision was made to allow the visit.

After that time, there were several instances of minor and adult victims requesting to visit their

predators. It's easy to make the decision to not let a minor visit, but is there really any difference between a child of seventeen and a child of eighteen, nineteen, or twenty years old when it comes to trauma? They're still victimized by the predator who continues to manipulate and interfere with their emotional development and self-esteem.

Another challenge to staff was the D-and-D (Dungeons and Dragons) group, whose general appearance and interest made them look like they were asking to be assaulted in prison. These were usually the soft, pasty, socially awkward sex offenders who were consumed with playing this fantasy game.

I'm not sure of the reason for the correlation between role-playing games such as D and D and this particular group of inmates. Research in this area would be interesting. It may be due to maturity level, compulsion to engage in fantasy, or other factors. But I think you'd find this is a common phenomenon at all sex-offender institutions.

These inmates generally appeared emotionally immature, weak, and physically unfit. Regardless of how staff felt about them, it was our job to look out for the safety of these inmates, even if the inmates were too naïve to look out for their own safety. Often, these same inmates, along with too

many others, had a penchant for drama. They'd engage in behavior that sent mixed messages to other inmates. When the other inmates responded to flirtation or conveyance of interest in a relationship, the drama nymph would run to others to be rescued. This would occur time and time again after they'd been in an agreed-upon sexual relationship. Staff then spent a great deal of time teasing out the facts. These inmates were cautioned repeatedly about the potential danger of their behavior; they were encouraged to participate in communication enhancement groups; they were moved to jobs where they could be more closely monitored; and they were generally encouraged by unit staff to make more constructive decisions.

CHAPTER 17: Prison Rape Elimination Act (PREA)

Karl was a young, black offender (not a sex offender) who appeared younger than his age and was slight of build. He was at Marion when I first arrived, when it was a supermax. Karl was housed in a single cell in one of the east corridor units. I became aware of him when some of the officers in his unit reported that he'd consistently stand at the front of the range next to the officers' station throughout the two hours of recreation.

Recreation alternated between outside rec and inside rec. During outside rec, eighteen inmates from one range could spend two hours outside in a small recreation pen enclosed with galvanized wire fencing. During inside rec, the cell doors would open and remain open. The eighteen inmates were free to come out on the range or remain in their cells. Inmates weren't allowed to be in one another's cell, but I'm sure this occurred. Officers maintained constant observation during rec. During inside rec, officers would sit at the end of the range and watch the inmates who were separated from him/her by a grille. The inmates

would usually exercise or play board games during this time.

The unit officers reported Karl would stand at the front of the range, sometimes silently and sometimes attempting to engage the officer in small talk. I met with him privately several times, asking in a variety of ways if he was having any problems on the range or in the unit. Karl was adamant that he was fine.

A few months later, I was contacted by an officer who stated Karl was "humping" the wall, seemingly unaware of his surroundings, while standing by the officers' station during recreation time. Karl was seen again in a private office on the unit, where he continued to maintain he was fine. However, he was distant and distracted this time. In the following weeks, he became less conversant. During rounds in the unit, he'd sit with a towel over his head as staff walked by. He refused to talk except to state, "I am a man."

Despite numerous efforts to establish rapport or increase a level of trust, he was becoming increasingly withdrawn and ill. Ultimately, he was transferred to a medical facility for psychiatric care. I strongly suspected this inmate was sexually assaulted, and the fear of the consequences of "snitching" was stronger than his need to protect his body or mental health.

The Prison Rape Elimination Act (PREA) was a strong force in the prison system. This Federal law was passed in 2003, but the standards on how it was to be enforced weren't issued until 2012. These standards applied to all prisons and jails. The focus of the law was to prevent, protect, and intervene on behalf of incarcerated individuals who were thought to be at risk of being raped. The standards also addressed appropriate treatment of an incarcerated individual who'd been the victim or perpetrator of a rape.

With the exception of the increased amount of paperwork and stress on staff, I saw only one major change in how we treated inmates as a result of this law. At all the institutions and for all the years I worked, staff had always been careful about the treatment of transgender inmates; had been responsive to the housing needs of young, small-statured, or otherwise vulnerable inmates; and had been attentive to reports of sexual assault. The occurrence of assault and attempted assault were rare; harassment was a little more common and allegations of such even more common.

Prior to the PREA standards, every accusation of sexual assault was investigated by staff who had the relevant information as opposed to being dictated by a universal policy. Each situation was different and handled accordingly. Just as there shouldn't be a mandated comprehensive response

every time an inmate states he's suicidal, there shouldn't be a definitive response every time there's an allegation of sexual assault. But with the issuance of the 2012 PREA standards, there was now a step-by-step procedure to be followed, including accompanying meetings and paperwork.

The biggest change with the enactment of PREA was the elimination of the easy option of placing the alleged victim in SHU. After PREA, it required approval from the warden and notification to the Central Office in DC. Prior to PREA, the inmate who made an allegation and the alleged assailant(s) would usually be placed in SHU until the situation could be investigated. Unfortunately, there were inherent risks in telling staff about an assault, be it sexual or otherwise. Unless staff felt confident there would be no repercussions from other inmates — which was rare — the victim was moved to SHU for his protection. Following the investigation, a decision would be made on the safest and most practical course of action.

From an outsider's perspective, it appears the victim's placement in SHU was punishment for being a victim. Thus, I certainly understand how someone who doesn't work in the prison system would want to impose a restriction on placing alleged victims of sexual assault in SHU. However, this well-intentioned but misguided decision could put an inmate in serious jeopardy.

Complaints of sexual assault became much more commonplace after we went through the mission change and with the institution of PREA standards. At our medium-security, sex-offender facility, an inmate was much less likely to be assaulted for snitching, especially if he snitched on another sex offender. False allegations were made due to vindictiveness or because of a coveted job or a desired cell. If an allegation was made, the accused was placed in SHU pending an investigation. If an inmate was upset with a staff member, an allegation meant the staff member would be reassigned, at least temporarily. The PREA standards provided another opportunity for inmates to manipulate the system.

In addition, there was an increased amount of consensual sexual activity and "relationships" with the new mission, consistent with what occurred in other sex-offender institutions (technically, there can be no consensual sex in prison, but I'm using this term to distinguish it from a sexual assault). In prison, with an increase in consensual sex comes an increase in allegations of sexual abuse. This is due to jealousy and the drama over relationships gone bad.

The more exhausting cases were those involving promiscuous homosexuals. They had a pattern of relationship "break-ups." The victim of the break-up would pursue his former partner, trying to

mend the relationship. The promiscuous partner would let staff know and make allegations about sexual harassment. Staff were compelled to investigate, again and again.

Some inmates — many of whom were in SHU for a variety of reasons — engaged in provocative behavior with other inmates, including sending sexually explicit notes to an inmate in an adjacent cell requesting a written response or a sample of their ejaculate on a cloth or piece of bread. If things didn't go well, the "victim" would produce evidence they were being harassed. Just a game of entrapment.

All of these things contribute to what can appear to be the BOP's failure to respond to allegations of sexual assault/harassment. Oftentimes, there's an agenda, and the allegation is false. If, by chance, it's true, it can be difficult to substantiate, similar to allegations in the community.

Occasionally, there were accusations of harassment (soliciting sex or sexual proposals) that were suspected to be valid, but harassment was also difficult to prove. In these cases, the inmates involved were moved to different units or jobs and the reports of harassment usually stopped. On a few occasions, we ended up transferring the alleged perpetrator due to multiple complaints. I sat in on a few investigations when interviews were conducted with the alleged perpetrator to ascertain

if he was indeed attempting to pressure other inmates into sex. I was always amazed by how convincing these inmates were in insisting they were being set up. Gestures, voice, eye contact, consistency in their stories — all very convincing.

Proponents in the LBGTQ community have had an impact on the treatment of transgender inmates in prison, resulting in a complicated situation. Historically, the BOP's policy was to maintain inmates in either male or female facilities depending on their degree of transition. If an inmate was taking hormones when he or she was sentenced, they were allowed to take hormones in the facility at their level of maintenance. Inmates weren't started on hormones while incarcerated. Those who were experiencing gender-identity dysphoria were seen by the psychology department on a routine basis.

In 2009, this policy changed. The new requirement is to match the standard of care in the community. So, inmates who've never received treatment can begin hormone treatment following a thorough evaluation and diagnosis as well as being allowed to continue the transition process.

Not surprisingly, there are a few inmates who claim to be transgender who are not. In at least two of these cases, the inmate had a severe personality disorder and this likely fulfilled his need for attention or excess contact with medical staff.

An additional complication is the community standard requiring inmates with the sex assignment of male and the gender identity of female to have "the real life experience" of living as women. In order for this to occur, transgender inmates have to be allowed to live as female within the male institution. They're issued bras, panties, and allowed to use the same products available to female inmates. If the institutions don't issue these items, many transgender inmates fabricate bras, panties, and make-up (markers, ink, colored drink-mix powder) despite the risk of being assaulted. Many behave in a more feminine manner than most females I know, which generates a great deal of interest from other inmates. This is clearly a safety issue. Allowing an anatomically male transgender inmate to indulge in feminine dress in a male facility, especially a sex-offender facility, seems unwise. Putting an inmate with male genitalia in a female institution seems equally unwise.

Marion was proactive with transgender inmates, responding by housing them in single cells at the front of the range, giving them high-visibility jobs, and counseling them frequently about safety issues. Most had short sentences, and although they wreaked a bit of havoc with their flamboyance and flirtations, none reported being sexually assaulted.

In twenty-four years, I counseled only two transgender inmates who seemed to have a full appreciation of their potentially dangerous situation. Both were very low-key in their efforts to identify as female. Behaviors that helped them hold on to their identity, such as underclothing and shaving their body, were done privately. They had long hair but kept it pulled back in a ponytail. They didn't flicker and flutter when they walked. They, in fact, acted as I would expect females to act if housed with predatory males.

One transgender inmate who was low-key, intelligent, and well-versed in litigation had a life sentence. He started hormone replacement therapy, was allowed female undergarments, and requested facial hair removal, voice lessons, and, eventually, sexual reassignment surgery (at taxpayers' expense). She was transferred to a female institution. Given the decree to match the standard of care to that in the community, to not do so means insensitivity and failure to treat a medical disorder, also known as deliberate indifference. It's a no-win situation for corrections and another challenge for correctional staff.

CHAPTER 18: Thou Shalt Not Kill

Given all the vicious assaults at Leavenworth and Marion supermax, it's surprising there weren't more deaths. Inmates could be stabbed twenty-five times or more and return from the hospital in a day or two. After the mission change, there was a significant decrease in the amount of violence on the compound. I suppose that's why it was so surprising when there was a homicide.

There were two Native American cellmates, both sex offenders. One was older and had a life sentence. He'd been incarcerated since he was eighteen years old and had been at Marion for a few years prior to the homicide. He'd successfully worked his way down the system; meaning, due to good behavior and length of time served, he could now be housed at a medium-security institution. His original crime was considered a sex offense, so he was sent to Marion as one of the "critical mass" transfers. This particular inmate wasn't very engaging but was polite enough, greeting staff in the hallways whenever he could.

One morning, immediately after the day-shift officer showed up, this inmate came up and asked the officer if they could talk. The officer took him

off the unit and into the hallway where it was quieter. The inmate then calmly asked the officer to cuff him because he'd just killed his cellmate. The officer sighed and, in a slightly scolding voice, said, "What did you do that for?" It would later come out that the inmate had waited for this officer to arrive for his shift to confess to him because he liked and trusted him.

The officer called for assistance via the radio and asked the first officer on the scene to check the cell. The younger officer went up to the cell to find the cellmate lying prone underneath a blanket with something resting on his chest, possibly a weapon. The officer carefully removed the blanket to find the twenty-three-year-old cellmate's intestines outside of his body. The officer said the intestines were arranged to look like a bouquet.

The assailant explained he and his cellmate had a disagreement. He'd knocked the cellmate out, but, after a few minutes, the cellmate started to get up, so he strangled him. To ensure he wouldn't get up again and that he was indeed dead, the assailant wanted to pull the cellmate's heart out. He said he cut too low and pulled the intestines out instead. He then cleaned up the cell.

The assailant was secured, the FBI was notified, the crime scene preserved, pictures were taken, the corpse was removed from the institution and memos were written.

I talked to the first responders perhaps two hours after the incident. The young officer who discovered the body worked in an adjacent unit. He was on his computer when I walked into his office. This was approximately three hours after he found the body. He looked up and gave an ordinary greeting. He was on the computer searching for the phone number of a plumber because he'd been having plumbing problems at his home. He seemed completely unaffected by his discovery a few hours previously. When questioned, he denied having any reaction to the event and indicated surprise at the idea he might. He was advised he may have delayed symptoms such as sleep disturbances or encroaching thoughts. Again, he expressed surprise at the idea this could even become an issue later. He gave the typical noble response, indicating this wasn't his first experience with violence.

The other officer, the one whom the assailant had confided in, was more seasoned. He had the same type of response. He indicated he'd been exposed to several violent incidents over the years and denied experiencing any reaction to the events earlier that day. What was most remarkable were the expressions on both their faces. These weren't leathery-faced men who were gritting their teeth, had distant stares and furrowed brows; nor were

they cold, detached, and robotic. Both men looked genuinely unaffected.

Most correctional officers are adamant about leaving their work at work. They claim to never talk about the events of the day with their family, partly to protect the family and partly because, well, they leave their work at work. I suspect some really were successful at compartmentalizing their experiences.

A few days after the homicide, by happenstance, the more experienced officer and two others were in my office. A conversation ensued regarding how difficult it was to be a correctional officer. According to these officers, the majority of their work was mundane and thankless. However, they must be ever ready for anything to transpire. When emergencies occur, it requires a detached but quick response; an emotional response makes the officer less effective. Good officers learn to inhibit all emotions. The seasoned officer explained this was the reason the gruesome murder of the young Native American in his unit had no impact on him.

However, the officer seemed to have had a revelation since we last spoke and was now distressed about his absence of distress. He went into detail about how detached and cold he'd become over the years, and how he was concerned that this had — or might — seep into his personal relationships.

This insightful officer also explained his theory about how officers compensate for the lack of fulfillment and emptiness they feel at work. His theory included ideas about officers collecting items outside of work to prove they matter and their work matters by displaying the fruit of their labors; i.e., money, muscles, women, boats, ATVs, cars, motorcycles, etc. Indeed, many officers seem to live beyond their means or seem to have complicated relationships — many women or many divorces. It's clearly unfulfilling work and yet so critical. Unfortunately, another consequence of their burden is widespread alcoholism, and even more troubling is the prevalence of suicide.

Officers can be trained to be adequate officers, but good officers have a quality that cannot be taught. This officer had that quality. This was a great officer, and even the murderous inmate knew it. The inmate knew this was the officer who'd appropriately handle any situation, even the most egregious.

Good officers are special. They rarely complain and consistently enforce the rules. Although inmates often grumble about these officers, they admit they feel most safe when these officers are on duty. They depend on these officers even though they're adversaries. A complicated and unusual relationship.

In contrast, there are officers who are rigid, believing nothing any inmate tells him or her and never giving it another thought. I don't have a great deal of respect for this type of officer, but I understand them. It's easy: Come to work, be consistent, and inmates know what to expect. These officers don't have to worry about being gamed. The downfall is they don't know what's going on in their unit, they don't cultivate information, and they don't respond to special needs such as inmates with intellectual deficits, medical issues, or psychiatric problems. Good officers know their inmates. They don't trust them, but they have a good sense of who they are: the shot-callers, the major manipulators, the manipulated, etc.

CHAPTER 19: Men o' War

After Marion's mission change in 2007, one of the units was converted into a Communications Management Unit (CMU). The CMU was established to restrict and track every outside communication an inmate has. Whereas all inmates can have their mail read and their telephone calls monitored, CMU inmates are always monitored.

There are two of these units in the Bureau of Prisons, and Marion's was the second after USP Terre Haute. The CMU is basically an institution within the institution. It's completely self-contained and has its own food service, recreation, and Special Housing Unit. Education, Medical, and Psychology comes to the unit to offer services. If a CMU inmate has an outside visitor, inmates in the rest of the institution are removed from the corridors so the CMU inmate can be moved to the visiting room. These inmates have absolutely no contact with inmates in the rest of the facility. The CMU unit can house up to fifty-four inmates.

Many of the inmates in the CMU are domestic or foreign terrorists, and others are individuals who, while incarcerated, continue to victimize people in

the community. Some pursue underage victims. Some compulsively attempt to run scams from prison on the unsuspecting in the community, and some compulsively contact and make threats to specific individuals in the community. Also, there are those who compulsively file false liens on law enforcement officers and government officials.

A few of the inmates at the Marion CMU were transferred from the ADX as a temporary step-down to a larger, open facility. Most of the ADX inmates seemed to appreciate the unit, given they had more freedom without having to deal with large groups of inmates. However, most of those in the CMU were quite disgruntled and either claimed to be innocent of all charges or minimized the potential harm of their behavior.

There was controversy related to this unit. Articles can be found on the internet suggesting the unit was shrouded in secrecy, referring to it as "Little Gitmo," or "Guantanamo North," and stating it was used to separate inmates who spoke out against the American government. There were lawsuits filed regarding the unconstitutionality of the CMUs because inmates weren't afforded due process before being placed on the unit and/or because of claims of discrimination. Several inmates accused the unit of targeting Muslims, maintaining there was a disproportionate number in the CMUs.

In an attempt to manage these inmates, their ability to contact anyone in the community, including family members, was more restricted and always closely monitored. Because all letters were read, including those in foreign languages, mail tended to be very slow. All phone calls had to be scheduled so they could be monitored by someone familiar with the language. There were no contact visits. The inmate and visitor(s) would be separat-ed by thick plexiglass and would speak to each other through the use of a telephone unit. The conversation was monitored by staff electronically.

The CMU was known by staff to be the most wearing. Many of the most outspoken individuals were the Muslim inmates, who tended to be extremely supportive of one another, so any interaction with one inmate quickly shifted to an interaction with a group of inmates. There seemed to be a tendency to interpret the enforcement of basic rules as targeting their religious beliefs. Thus, reaction to a simple request or order could quickly escalate.

I don't want to give the impression that all the Muslim inmates banded together. There were a few on the unit who were outside the mainstream. They presented themselves as consistently emotionally balanced, almost sage-like, as if they truly embraced their religious teachings, as opposed to those who were more radical. Sure, some had

participated in horrendous acts of terror and some were found guilty of providing support to terrorists. But, on the unit, their behavior was respectful. One of the most respectful inmates on the unit had shot five people while on a grounded hijacked airplane and thrown them out of the plane. Two died. I suppose this was his response to failed negotiations. Most people would have difficulty believing this thoughtful, soft spoken, polite, insightful man was a terrorist who spurred a hijacking fiasco that resulted in the death of 58 passengers and crew members.

Several members of the Sovereign Citizen movement also proved to be a challenge to manage. Sovereign Citizens were considered to be anti-government extremists who believed the laws of the U.S. government were no longer valid. There were Sovereign Citizens throughout the Bureau of Prisons, and the CMUs housed those that were considered most problematic for the community. These individuals espoused complicated arguments regarding the government, currency, copyright notifications, security agreements, and power of attorney. Their explanations were excessively detailed, lengthy, and marked by inaccurate interpretation of facts. I could have listened to them talk for hours and not understood anything they said. They were known for "paperwork terrorism," filing so many documents

and arguing for so long, even on the most inane issues, they simply exhausted their opponent.

The unit also seemed to have more than its fair share of individuals who considered themselves much smarter than anyone else. They'd explain their interpretation of the Constitution or some esoteric law that would/should absolve them of their crime or any infraction. They inundated staff with administrative paperwork, with many inmates filing the same complaint, which required as many responses. It was clear they were less interested in getting an answer than in using the system to hound and provoke.

Decisions regarding who was placed in CMU and who could transfer out of CMU weren't made at the institutional level. One of the understandable sources of frustration for the inmates was the lack of clear criteria for transferring out of the unit. Sometimes, model inmates were denied and provocateurs were approved for transfer to the larger compound. It really was difficult to understand, both for inmates and for staff that worked on the unit.

The most interesting inmates were those who had horrendous histories or were constantly trying to run a scam, compromise staff, or circumvent security. They could have been the subject of a *Saturday Night Live* skit, highlighting blatant lack of self-awareness. They continuously expected to be

transferred and would have a meltdown every time they were denied.

CHAPTER 20: A Plethora of Hidden Agendas

In addition to working with inmates who straight up engage in misconduct, there's the challenge of working with inmates who are conniving, deceitful, and devious. There's no indicator to help staff discern which inmates are manipulative and which are not. To communicate with inmates, especially at the higher security levels, it's necessary to constantly be aware of the latent content of the conversation. Some inmates seem to communicate in code. In these cases, specifics are never used and rarely are proper nouns; the inmate uses pronouns, at best. This is another symptom of not being able to accept responsibility. There's also the ever-present inmate who provides information to staff, gaining staff members' trust, and then playing off this trust to further engage in wrongful behavior.

Other inmates tend to be demanding, impulsive, and impatient. An inmate who has intestinal gas can demand to be seen by medical staff as earnestly as an inmate with chest pains and a history of heart disease. When inmates are experiencing some type of minor distress, they demand to be seen by a department head immediately and, if this doesn't occur, they claim to be suicidal.

Another popular demand relates to the use of restraints. Inmates complain about restraints being too tight when they're often not. I've heard inmates scream as if they're in terrible pain when they were the subject of a forced cell move. Later, they laugh about it. And the statement, "I can't breathe," has become synonymous with The Boy Who Cried Wolf.

Here's an example of drama relating to the process of restraint. While in SHU, an inmate had covered the front of his cell with a blanket so he wasn't visible to staff and stated he planned to kill himself. An immediate use of force was initiated. When staff ran into his cell to restrain him, the inmate began yelling that they were breaking his leg. The staff were, in fact, lying on him as they attempted to apply restraints. This inmate had a history of assaulting staff, and the staff proceeded with their endeavor until he was properly restrained. The inmate continued to maintain his ankle was hurt. He was x-rayed and examined. There appeared to be no injury. The next day he was recreating.

For those of you who feel outraged when you see videotapes of law-enforcement officers seeming to be indifferent when a person in restraints claims to be in distress, it's because of the multitude of times these claims are falsely made. The tragedy is that sometimes the person is genuinely in distress or

injured. On the other hand, if staff loosened their hold every time they heard these protests, they would themselves be injured, or worse.

Some inmates will, due to anger or a desire to prove a point, actually use restraints to cause self-injury. When an inmate is placed in hand restraints, the restraints can be locked to ensure they don't tighten. If they're not locked, pressure on the restraint can cause it to cut off circulation. Normally, officers will lock the restraint, but if a SHU inmate is just being escorted to a shower or recreation, this security measure is sometimes disregarded.

A particularly contentious inmate, who had a long history of running scams — both inside and outside of prison — refused to allow an officer to remove his handcuffs after being escorted from the shower back to his cell. The inmate tightened the handcuffs and stated he was willing to cause nerve damage to his hands just to get transferred out of the facility. The inmate continuously orchestrated scenarios like this — situations that couldn't be ignored. He'd feign medical issues, threaten suicide, and continuously required an audience. This inmate was eventually transferred to the ADX. He'd been a CMU inmate and had exhausted all his housing options. He didn't require the security level of the ADX but he did require a high level of communication restrictions. This particular

inmate served several sentences for being a "con man." He was apparently not very good at it.

In addition to having to deal with inmates that are dangerous and manipulative, there are the arrogant, condescending, highbrow variety. Correctional officers aren't hired because they're scholars, sages, or magnates. They're hired to enforce rules; make sound, safe decisions; and act appropriately in an emergency situation. That isn't to say many aren't well-read or college-educated, but solving philosophical problems or revamping federal policies isn't in their job description.

Despite this, there are inmates who look for any opportunity to present their lofty ideas and instruct staff on better ways to run the range, unit, facility, or planet. They have a point to make, so they want their voice heard. These are often the inmates who become prolific writers. They write administrative remedies for themselves and others. They write to the regional offices, the central office, and their congressional represent-atives, which is certainly their right to do. Via friends or family, they post their complaints and observations on the internet. Often these postings are a compelling read because of their interesting phraseology, but they aren't necessarily accurate.

CHAPTER 21: Learned Helplessness

In addition to the frustration and difficulty in working with inmates, there are the perplexing events that occur — those things that simply can't be understood. One example came in 2005 when two inmates assaulted two staff members in one of the new, bigger units. At that time, Marion was a supermax and this particular unit was being used as a transition unit. These inmates had more freedom. Unlike the non-transitional units where inmates were observed during recreation by an officer in a secured area, in the transitional unit, two officers were present on the unit when inmates were out of their cells.

After a verbal exchange between an inmate and an officer, an inmate punched the officer and knocked him out. When the other officer ran to assist, he was sucker punched by the second inmate. He suffered a serious brain injury after being spun around and hitting his head on the concrete wall. The next day, the assailants were moved to a different institution for their own protection. Whenever staff are seriously assaulted and there's concern about retaliation, it's standard

procedure for inmates to be immediately moved to another facility.

At the receiving institution, the two inmates complained about their treatment following their assault on staff. Although it couldn't be substantiated, nine staff members were accused of retaliating against the inmates immediately after the incident. Some were accused of assaulting the inmates, some were accused of witnessing the assault and not intervening, and some were accused of seeing the injuries from the assault and not reporting it. The staff members were disciplined by being given unpaid leave, being forced to take positions at other facilities, or being fired. All three correctional staff that were fired, after appealing their cases, were reinstated. With the exception of wreaking havoc with these staff members' personal and professional lives for years, nothing came of this. There was no conclusive evidence the inmates had been abused.

Meanwhile, both inmates were awarded a substantial out-of-court settlement — that's taxpayers' money. Most amazing? The inmates were never prosecuted for the assault. The blatant lack of support for staff and apparent support of the inmates in the face of witnessed and video-recorded evidence of the assault on staff...well, it's just perplexing.

A few years later, an inmate approached me and stated he needed to discuss something very important with the warden privately. He made it clear he couldn't be seen speaking with her, and he requested my help. This was an unusual scenario. There have been plenty of times an inmate who is upset demands to see the warden, but this wasn't the case here. He was calm. He was clearly requesting help in being discreet. Usually when inmates have "information," they request assistance in speaking to a lieutenant or the captain. I knew this was important. I contacted the warden, and a meeting took place that day in my office.

The inmate stated he'd seen a correctional officer in one of the units provide pornographic images of children to an inmate — a sex-offending inmate. The reporting inmate gave details about walking into the officers' station and witnessing a specific inmate sitting with the officer as they looked at images on the computer. The inmate was convincing, and the information was easy to verify.

Immediately following our conversation, the warden had the computer in the unit officer's office confiscated. A scan of the computer supported the inmate's allegation.

To protect the reporting inmate, he was emergently transferred to another facility that day. The alleged recipient of the images was placed in

SHU and later transferred to another facility. The staff member? Well, he wasn't prosecuted! He was retirement-eligible and was allowed to retire — with full benefits. Ironically, this officer had been a champion at finding pornography in inmates' cells for the previous couple of years. It never occurred to us that he might be the supplier.

The U.S. Attorney's Office is in charge of making the decision to prosecute in such a case — if they'd been made aware of the situation. I have no idea where the decision was made, but I suspect the intention was to avoid publicity and embarrassment for the Bureau. This isn't really so perplexing, but it's quite sickening.

Good staff struggle each and every day with the inconsistencies inherent in their line of work: staff need to be disciplined and aren't, staff are rewarded and shouldn't be, staff are assigned difficult tasks and rise to the occasion but receive no acknowledgement. Others do nothing and go without reprimand. In the Bureau of Prisons, it's nearly impossible to terminate staff. Toxic or lazy staff that aren't receptive to supervision are promoted and transferred as the only resolution to problems. Imagine the feeling of those who watch this show. When correctional staff get hired, they believe in the system. It doesn't take long for this to falter. This element of the system is broken in so many ways.

CHAPTER 22: Hippocrates Had No Idea

Inmates are expected to receive healthcare services in a manner consistent with accepted community standards. This causes some complicated situations in the BOP. To ensure adequate care, mainstream correctional facilities (as opposed to medical facilities) contract with specialists in the community. Specialists rarely come to the facility; instead, inmates are taken to the specialist. Thus, frequent trips are made to local clinics and physicians' offices, which causes significant financial and time constraints on both medical and custody staff. Risks of escape or introduction of contraband increases with each trip.

There's also the general frustration among the institution medical staff with inmates who refuse to comply with treatment — in particular, those with diabetes who often end up requiring a great deal of outside attention. These inmates frequently don't monitor their blood-sugar levels, refuse to control their diet, and refuse to participate in an exercise program, which results in worsening of their condition and the need for visits to specialists.

Complicating the treatment of inmates with real medical concerns is the intertwining of an

abundance of inmates who are drug-seeking, theatrical, and attention-seeking; trying to be in a secluded area with female staff; wanting to be in an air-conditioned room during the summer; wanting to get out of work; wanting a lower bunk pass; or are interested in planning avenues for an escape.

In general, it seems that manipulative inmates often target health-services staff. I imagine it has something to do with the idea that those in a helping profession are more caring and more vulnerable. At the higher-security facilities, it doesn't take long for compassionate staff to quit, be compromised, or become hardened. Hence, inmates commonly complain about their treatment by medical staff in the BOP. The vast majority of medical staff treat inmates' medical problems adequately but usually do so with indifference or even disdain. Many develop a level of sarcasm and distance that allows them to do their job while clearly conveying they're not interested in being manipulated or serving as the source of fantasies. In a correctional facility, it's impossible to know an inmate's motivations. It's safer and much more efficient to just attend to the health of the inmate without the compassion that might be seen in the community.

The downside of this is inmates are able to amass sympathy from those in the community and outside the facility regarding the apparent cold-

heartedness of medical staff in the facility. That, compounded by the fact there have been a few highly publicized incidents of medical staff who were found guilty of malpractice at correctional facilities, leads to a false impression that there's widespread incompetence. There is not.

Much of the medication provided to inmates has to be controlled due to concerns about overdose or misuse. Thus, inmates are required to attend "pill line." At most facilities, this means medication is distributed at specific times during the day to every inmate who requires it. Usually, there's at least an early morning, midday, and evening line where large groups of inmates are released from their unit to take their medication. At Marion, this seemed to have always been an experience of great distress for inmates and staff.

Marion medical staff crushed all medications (unless prohibited) and gave them with a small cup of water or with the medication in the water. Inmates hated that. Most complained about the taste. Some refused it. The staff preferred to administer the medication this way. The alternative would have been to check their mouths to circumvent anyone "cheeking" the medication. Apparently, cheeking medication is relatively easy.

Like most facilities that had more than one mission, pill lines occurred in multiple places at different times during the day. At Marion, the

same person conducted the pill line for the main facility, SHU, the camp, and the CMU. That meant there were twelve pill lines conducted each day. One pill line could take up to ninety minutes at the main facility. Therefore, some of the pill lines had to be conducted early in order to allow time for all of them. Inmates complained about the timing of pill lines, especially those individuals that were taking sedating medication early in the evening. They also didn't like the medication being distributed at movie or recreation time, but it was unavoidable.

There were several lawsuits brought against health-services staff during the time I was employed at Marion. I'm positive some of these were painstakingly fabricated, created over years of feigning falls or paralysis. There was an inmate who was adamant he was unable to walk and crawled from his cell to the shower for years or insisted he needed a wheelchair, yet he was captured on video dancing and standing on his bunk.

Some of the more interesting medical challenges were the few inmates who insisted they required adult diapers but who had no medical need of these. One inmate transferred in with a diagnosis of neurogenic bladder. He was routinely provided adult diapers by the hospital staff. After closely reviewing his file, it was also discovered he had a

diagnosis of paraphilic infantilism — a condition in which the individual is sexually aroused by being treated like a baby.

Another inmate who insisted he needed adult diapers due to incontinence also periodically insisted he needed to be catheterized because he was unable to urinate. When he was catheterized, there was no urine. He also insisted he suffered from coprophagia, that is, eating feces — his own. There was absolutely no doubt he was lying and just wanted to have the attention of medical staff. His reported coprophagia quickly resolved when he was told he'd receive an incident report for being unsanitary.

I can't emphasize enough how difficult it is to attend to the medical needs — legitimate and otherwise — of this population.

CHAPTER 23: USP Bedlam

The deinstitutionalization of the mentally ill during the 1970s and 1980s was partially driven by concerns about patient's rights and partially motivated by the Government's desire to get themselves out of the business of psychiatric care. The goal was to move care from mental health hospitals to community clinics. The intention was good, but the follow-through was poor. The community clinics didn't receive the needed financial support, and the mentally ill ended up being released from substandard hospitals to the streets, where they got no treatment. Over time, the lack of care for the mentally ill in the community had a direct impact on the Bureau of Prisons. Many of these individuals ended up being incarcerated.

Attending to mental-health needs in a prison environment is quite a challenge. For inmates who are clearly ill, individual, group, and pharmaceutical treatment is provided. But, because of the variety of characters one finds in prison, it's sometimes difficult to discern who's mentally ill and who isn't. Having access to the presentence investigation report (PSR), which is

composed by a probation officer for the court, is an advantage. It usually contains detailed information about personal, medical, and mental-health history along with other information. Inmates who have verified, documented histories of treatment are attended to accordingly.

Occasionally, the PSR is based on an inmate's self-reporting and records aren't verified or are deceiving. One inmate who had numerous brief hospitalizations for a variety of diagnoses, insisted he needed a variety of medications. Upon closer review, it became apparent he was a homeless substance abuser. When the weather was bad or when he had psychotic symptoms from overuse of drugs, he'd check in to a psychiatric hospital for a couple of days and then check out. We attempted to provide him with new coping skills so he could stay out of SHU and participate in drug treatment programming, but he wasn't receptive to this idea.

There are, of course inmates who manage to go undiagnosed prior to incarceration or develop a disorder while incarcerated. Diagnoses are made more complicated due to the number of inmates who present with unusual symptom patterns, perhaps due to traumatic brain injuries (TBI) from their violent past or complications of extensive substance abuse histories. There are young inmates who are first diagnosed with schizophrenia while incarcerated and older

inmates who develop dementia. There are inmates who suffer from schizophrenia, brief psychotic disorder, delusional disorder, autism, depression, anxiety disorders, obsessive-compulsive disorder, body dysmorphic disorder, and of course, substance abuse and paraphilic (deviant sexual desire) disorders.

In addition, diagnoses are complicated by those who feign illness for secondary gain or because of psychopathic complications. Just to clarify, a psychopath is a remorseless predator who doesn't respond positively to mental-health interventions. In fact, mental-health treatment can actually provide them with additional tools for victimizing others, thus doing more harm than good. For this reason, informed clinicians do their best to keep these characters out of treatment groups, where they're able to gather tidbits of information about others that they can use to prey on them.

In attempting to discern the *Who's Who* in the psychiatric prison playbook, more than reported and observed symptoms have to be considered. An inmate who intentionally cuts himself might be relieving stress, attempting to gain sympathy, engaging in a suicide gesture, or having impulse and anger management issues — all potential symptoms of a mental-health disorder. However, he may just want a cell change, enjoy the shock-and-awe value of his act, have a communicable

disease he wants to share with an officer, or be violent and have absolutely no regard for anyone, including himself — all potential symptoms of psychopathy.

There are countless inmates who report auditory or visual hallucinations with absolutely no other symptoms, including an absence of a visceral reaction, thought disorder, or behavioral impact. There are inmates who go to great lengths to mimic a disorder or fabricate a new-and-improved disorder just because they delight in duping people. For this reason, staff are skeptical when an inmate who's been incarcerated for several years and has no history of mental illness or recent head injury seemingly wakes up one day and is psychotic. However, there was that one instance.

A Hispanic inmate had apparently engaged in a serious faux pas during the week and was told by fellow gang members a "hit" had been placed on him. The reality of this situation and the intense fear and stress caused a brief psychotic reaction. He was so scared he lost contact with reality. Seemingly overnight, he became suicidal (it's better to kill yourself quickly than to deal with the unknown of when and how someone else will kill you), delusional, and was having both visual and auditory hallucinations. He clearly wasn't playing. He was immediately placed on suicide watch and closely monitored.

This was the only inmate I ever encountered who was able to destroy the very expensive suicide blankets and smocks that are marketed as indestructible. He ripped up the material, wrapped pieces around his head like a Russian Ushanka hat and around his torso to look like a chest shield, and then sat and intently watched his hallucinations stroll back and forth in front of his cell. I'm sure this is what Attila the Hun looked like when glowering at enemies. We immediately replaced his cloth safety smock with a paper hospital gown. It was easier than dealing with Attila's destruction and risking suicide by safety blanket. Ultimately, this inmate agreed to take an anti-psychotic medication. Once his thinking cleared, the delusions subsided, he was moved to a new unit (where none of his gang members resided). To my knowledge, this was his only mental-health episode.

Sometimes, serious mental-health symptoms can't be managed with medication or the inmate refuses medication and deteriorates to a level where he can no longer function in our facility. Usually, it's obvious when this occurs. Other inmates express concern or the affected inmate is so disruptive to the orderly running of the institution that he's placed in SHU before he becomes violent or on suicide watch before he engages in serious self-harm.

If all attempts to help the inmate fail and he can't safely remain in our facility due to mental-health issues, a request for transfer to a medical facility is submitted. Medical facilities rarely had psychiatric beds available. They tried to accommodate the most severely mentally ill. This meant some inmates who were very ill — but not as ill as others — were denied transfer. Even if they were approved for transfer, it could take weeks before they were actually moved.

Inmates with serious mental-health disorders, such as bi-polar mood disorder or schizophrenia, were usually managed in general population as long as they were on their medication. If stable, we'd attempt to house them in a single cell on a smaller, quiet unit. If they had a cellmate, care went into the selection of that cellmate. Care was also taken with work assignments. Unit staff were responsive when working with most of the mentally ill.

Some inmates were clearly mentally ill and refused to take medication but were able to continue to be on the compound. These inmates had delusions but weren't disruptive. One inmate occasionally wore underwear on his head or Band-aids all over his body. A few inmates would chassé (dance) up and down the hallways but were allowed to remain on the compound as long as they were functioning well enough. One inmate, who had a

severe cognitive disorder, would twirl, moon walk, flail his arms, and constantly move in odd and intriguing ways. He was adamant he didn't need medication.

Most staff easily understand and respond appropriately if an inmate is severely mentally ill. Most custody staff work closely with psychology staff to ensure these inmates attend to their activities of daily-living (dressing, eating, toileting, etc.). Staff are tolerant when these inmates have poor hygiene or engage in misconduct and work with the inmate as much as possible to help them function within the environment.

Inmates who don't demonstrate extreme symptoms of mental illness are the most challenging for staff, especially if they're manipulative. This includes inmates with intellectual deficits, autism-spectrum disorder, or attention-deficit disorder. These cause conceptualization problems.

In my experience at Marion, many staff members held fast to the idea that mental illness and manipulation were mutually exclusive. Thus, some of these inmates were thought to be "faking," which led staff to be less tolerant. On these occasions, discussions would ensue regarding the benefit of understanding that inmates can be both ill and manipulative. Sometimes, this was successful; sometimes, not so much.

There were also inmates who engaged in unique odd behaviors. One insisted on consuming con-coctions made of rancid food he collected and fermented (with an absence of yeast, so it wasn't hooch). Despite being counseled numerous times by several people about the health risks of this activity, he continued to stow away food, mix it into a soupy mush, and let it stew for days and weeks. Another inmate performed liposuction on himself, using a fingernail or paperclip to cut himself, a plastic spoon to scoop his fat, and put it into a cup. He focused primarily on his hips. The inmate wasn't overweight but had a history of obesity. One inmate refused to quit sitting in the sun and had constant second-degree burns on his face and head. We provided him with sunblock and a hat, but he wouldn't comply. Eventually, his thoughts became significantly confused and we were successful in getting him transferred to a medical facility.

Psychiatric services (prescribing medication for mental illness) have been handled in different ways at different institutions and differently over time. Medical facilities and other select facilities like the transfer center in Oklahoma have psychiatrists on staff. General population institutions usually do not, so they sometimes contract with a psychiatrist in the community and sometimes used telepsychiatry. Telepsychiatrists are BOP psychiatrists who meet with inmates via

a secure technology system. Some institutions use the institution physician for psychiatric services.

When I started at Marion, telepsychiatric services were provided on a routine basis by the Federal Medical Center Springfield. Springfield provided this service only to high security institutions, so when Marion transitioned to a medium-security facility, this changed. We had periods in which we had no psychiatrist available, periods where we had telepsychiatrists available from other medical facilities, and a brief period of using contract psychiatrists. Although, in theory, it's better to have a psychiatrist available in person to provide services, it turned out to be the least useful option for us. In addition to the added expense, local psychiatrists didn't understand the importance of attending to malingering and manipulation.

A. Barren, a small, Native American inmate who had a long history of mental illness marked with hallucinations and paranoid delusions — most often involving females and resulting in sexual offenses — had been on medication to help curb some of the delusions. Barren wanted to discontinue medication. Although we couldn't force compliance with medication, we always found it easier to try to convince an inmate to remain on medication than to convince him to get back on medication once it was stopped. Our interventions

usually involved the use of encouragement to continue the medication and attempting to address reasons for wanting to discontinue; i.e., side effects.

When Barren was brought to see the contract psychiatrist because he was complaining about side effects and didn't like attending the pill line, he told her he didn't know why he was on Haldol, an antipsychotic medication. He denied any psychiatric issues. So she stopped the prescription. As eerie and menacing as he was even when taking the medication, she ensured an inevitable decline in functioning and increased the chances of an assault on female staff. It was our good fortune, in some disturbing way, that prior to any harm to staff, Barren pissed off another inmate who assaulted him, resulting in his placement in the Special Housing Unit. He was eventually transferred to a medical facility. We never saw him again.

A. Mondo was a quiet, large, black inmate in his early twenties who was housed in general population. When he came to USP Marion, he had no known serious mental health issues. Some mental illnesses don't present until adulthood. Mondo had been at Marion for several months when he gradually began to display symptoms of mental illness. He was adamant he was going to be released soon, despite his thirty-year sentence. He was convinced his mother and other family

members were speaking to him through the radio. He was chronically angry, confused, and distressed. He refused to follow rules and continued to deteriorate. He also refused medication, thus a request for transfer to a medical facility was submitted and accepted.

Following successful treatment at the medical center, Mondo was transferred back. He could have been a poster child for the benefits of psychotropic medication. Not only were his hallucinations and delusions gone, his thoughts were clearer and more focused and his emotions were more fluid. His eyes were brighter and his face was more expressive and pleasant. He smiled more and was generally more personable. Mondo had no idea how ill he'd been.

When he immediately started voicing his intention to discontinue his medication, he was reminded of his previous behavior. He was also encouraged, cajoled, and warned. This worked for a short while, but then he stopped taking his medication.

Weeks later, Mondo was on the range in his unit with the rest of the inmates when they were all told recreation was over and it was time to lock up. All complied except Mondo. Officers tried to reason with him prior to contacting the Lieutenant's Office. The lieutenant came to the unit and attempted to gain compliance. Mondo stood in the middle of the range and refused to comply. A forced

cell team was assembled. Less-than-lethal munitions were used, also to no avail. Sting balls might as well have been spit balls, and pepper balls (small projectiles filled with pepper spray that explode on impact) also had no effect. Mental illness sometimes causes superhuman responses and reactions, plus Mondo was using a large bath mat to shield himself.

The bath mat was one of those many things inmates request to make their living situation more comfortable. A bath mat meant they didn't have to use one of their towels to dry their feet prior to walking out of the shower and down the range. Now it was being used by an inmate to circumvent safety and security.

The five correctional officers on the forced cell team entered the range to take down this psychotic, adrenaline-fueled individual. Despite the odds, staff fought for several minutes before gaining control of Mondo. One staff member admitted that he was worried they wouldn't be successful. Mondo was ridiculously strong.

Some inmates with intellectual deficits and those with fetal alcohol syndrome also proved to be particularly challenging. Both are vulnerable to predators, but they also tend to not follow unwritten prison rules. They're more likely to non-discreetly snitch, walk in front of inmates watching television, or be unintentionally disrespectful. In

addition, they're less likely to respond to staff instructions appropriately due to a lack of understanding or poor impulse control.

Consistent with the community at large, the most difficult group to work with are those with personality disorders. They take up a great deal of staff's attention due to chronic interpersonal difficulties, emotional lability, and impulsivity. It takes a village to manage these inmates.

There have been institutions that attempted to establish special programs to help alleviate the burden of personality disordered inmates. The success of these programs seems to depend on many factors including having staff that can tolerate the strain, management willing to provide enough staff, and an ability to weed out those inmates that don't respond to any type of treatment.

When I was an intern, one of my supervisors gave me this pearl of wisdom: "There are two kinds of inmates who are seen by psychology services — those that are in pain and those that are a pain. Choose to spend most of your time with the former."

It is not always easy to tell the difference.

CHAPTER 24: Dirty Staff

I doubt there are very many staff members who hire into the Bureau of Prisons with the intent of having sex with an inmate or bringing in contraband as a get-rich scheme. Inmates watch staff and know who's vulnerable. Of the staff that were compromised whom I personally knew, in hindsight, only one was a surprise. Three staff members ended up doing prison time for their behavior, which included bringing in drugs and providing false information. I personally knew four female staff accused of having sexual relations with male inmates. In every case, the staff members had poor communication patterns with inmates. They tended to yell at or belittle inmates as if they (the staff) had poor boundaries and had to keep inmates at a far distance simply to maintain any boundary at all. Each was befriended by a specific and different inmate. Each was counseled early on about her relationship with the inmate. All were highly defensive and ignored interventions.

In fact, while I was in the middle of writing this book, another female staff member at Marion, one I worked with for several years, was escorted out of the institution and restricted from re-entering the

facility while she was being investigated. She was eventually charged with bringing in contraband to an inmate. She also interfered with the investigation by lying to authorities. I don't think any of the staff who knew her were surprised. The general consensus was she was permeable, her boundaries were poor. The implied theory is, over the eleven years she worked for the government, she hadn't changed or become more vulnerable. It had simply taken that long for her to be compromised — or caught.

A male staff member that I supervised always seemed a little too sympathetic when it came to inmates. He was quick to side with an inmate and more than once confronted me with an inmate in tow after he'd been advised several times to discuss issues with staff privately. When he began to have personal and financial problems, an inmate was able to convince him to bring cocaine into the institution. The inmate eventually was fitted with a wire and the staff member was indicted.

In all of these cases, it was so easy for an outsider to see the manipulation but so difficult for the target to see it.

In addition to staff being compromised, there were staff who walked or crossed the line. One staff member, who never actually violated any policy, repeatedly antagonized entire units. He'd arbitrarily pick cells to shake down, as he should,

but he'd confiscate items he knew would most bother the inmates, such as fans during the summer. Inmates were required to have their registration number on all their property. If they failed to update the number on their fan, technically the fan shouldn't be in their cell. Inmates eventually got their fans back, but it was a hassle for both inmates and supervisors.

This type of staff member caused extra work for other staff. There were days where it felt like all I did was fix issues staff members created. The value in having worked at the same facility for a long time was knowing which staff were reputable and which were provocateurs. When inmates complained about staff, I had a good sense of whether the complaint was valid. It was interesting that inmates rarely complained about officers who enforced the rules. Most complaints were made about those that were inconsistent, those that were condescending, and those that let inmates get away with breaking rules.

CHAPTER 25: Stress Management

When I hired into the BOP, there was a unit manager and a case manager who were planning on retiring within the next year. Both were, well, crazy. The unit manager was a Vietnam vet and yelled at inmates about a war that had ended fifteen years prior. The case manager stuck every piece of gum he chewed behind his ear and had collected a wad by the end of the day.

On my first day at Leavenworth, a cantankerous officer who was retiring in a few months started spitting and sputtering at me in the middle of the center hall about how he "hated fucking newbies." He mistakenly thought I was a rookie because I'd asked directions. I sometimes worried I'd become like these guys when I was close to retirement. Were they crazy when they started, or did the BOP make them crazy?

I've now concluded that these guys, and many more like them, had lost their sense of humor. A sense of humor is the only way to survive the journey in corrections. The best medicine was laughter and, for correctional staff, that usually meant laughing at other people. There was an unusual sense of humor that united staff, and there

were no secrets. Of course, almost everything we did was captured on a closed-circuit camera, so if you fell walking up the steps but were able to somehow do it without spilling your coffee, it was recorded and later played for anyone who walked in the Lieutenant's Office. An amazingly controlled fall. Caricatures and pictures with inappropriate humorous depictions were posted frequently.

I could walk by the Lieutenant's Office on any given day and a group of staff would be gathered around a monitor laughing at some violent interchange between two inmates, expressing joy when an inmate landed a particularly good swing on a person of larger stature. Staff would sit and laugh about the most disturbing things. They chortled when talking about how a staff member acted when they were assaulted with a cocktail of water, urine and feces; or how they acted when they were exposed to tear gas. Although this sense of humor was disturbing at one level, it seemed to serve an adaptive purpose. Without it, staff seemed to wither.

Some staff made the most out of every situation that presented itself. When the Activity Lieutenant caught a bird that had come through the office window, he stuck it in the desk drawer of the Operations Lieutenant and waited for him to start his shift. When the Ops Lieutenant finally arrived and settled behind his desk, the Activity

Lieutenant asked the Ops for the stapler in his drawer.

A live mouse was carefully pried from a sticky trap and then placed under a paper cup atop an "important" document in a mailbox. When the paper was removed from the overhead box, the mouse jumped onto the staff member's head and ran down to his shoulder. Because of the stickiness on its feet, the mouse became stuck there while the staff member jumped around, attempting to dislodge the rodent.

There were endless pranks and tasteless jokes, especially when reviewing particularly gory videos of inmate fights. Clever staff were always able to create puns, posters, or pithy remarks.

There was the lieutenant who was having problems with his new Harley Davidson motorcycle leaking oil and took it in to be serviced. On the day he picked it up, he rode it to work. Once he was inside, a correctional officer, in cahoots with another lieutenant, poured dirty oil over the gasket and underneath the motorcycle. Another officer then came in and told the Harley owner his bike was leaking oil all over the place. The lieutenant flew out the door to check on his bike with the pranksters in tow, who watched the fireworks with glee. Eventually he was told about the trick, but not until he'd yelled, cursed, grumbled, and

stretched out on the ground in his uniform to investigate the apparent malfunction.

Before I retired, I received an email from a staff member with whom I rarely communicated. We worked in different areas and just didn't need to interact. He'd started as a correctional officer and had been promoted to heating venting/air conditioning (HVAC) supervisor. I assume he found it entertaining whenever staff members that had collateral duties listed all their job titles on emails and documents, because he decided to list every job position, collateral duty, and anything else he'd ever done in the institution on the bottom of all his emails, which I've included at the end of this chapter. In addition to finding it humorous, I was amazed at the list. I suspect most of the older correctional officers in the institution would have a similar list. Being an officer is so much more than just sitting in one unit watching inmates.

This particular employee had worked in the control center. He'd worked in the control unit when Marion was the only supermax, before ADX Florence opened. He'd worked in the towers. He'd operated the L8, which is the machine that launches the less-than-lethal munitions. He'd worked as a corridor officer. He'd supervised inmates recreating and handed out laundry, food trays, toilet paper, and supplies. He'd participated on forced cell teams and worked in the message

center, which controlled entry into the institution when it was a supermax. He'd kept track of inmate property when individuals were sent to SHU. He'd participated on the Disturbance Control Team, which is a specially trained group of staff who are called in for large-scale disturbances.

There has reportedly been a ghost in every institution where I've worked. At Marion, the ghost had a name, Omar. He was thought to live in the old unit above Health Services. Apparently, this staff member had an interaction with Omar, as you will see him referenced in the HVAC supervisor's list of jobs, duties, and locations:

HVAC supervisor
Control Center #1
Control Unit #1
Control Unit #8
D-unit #2, evening watch
C-unit #2, evening
G-unit #3
Seg #4, evening watch
B-unit #2, evening watch
F-unit #3
4 tower officer
L8 operator
Baton specialist
East corridor officer
Rec officer

Forced cell team technician
Inmate compliance specialist
Message center operator
Tea cart specialist
Property specialist
Gas gun specialist
Disturbance Control Team member
Special laundry passer
Professional radio transmitter
Key passer-outer
Transition prison specialist
A/C guy
Fridge guy
Tool guy
Crap-thrown-on guy
Yard-walker guy
Food cart guy
Supply passer guy
Property box guy
Hospital escort guy
Food tray passer-out guy
Toilet paper passer guy
Aaaaahhh Omar!!!
Lock box operator guy
Shower escort
Open 5 cell guy
Gym rec guy
Tunnel inspector guy
Bus-shoe-wearing guy

Hot water guy
Ice bucket guy
Hockey helmet guy
Help-force-feed guy
Red body-alarm guy
Leg iron professional guy
Nope-you-ainta-going-to-get-it guy
Somebody-fell-in-a-hole guy
Please-turn-my-water-on guy
Clearance-on-seg-door guy
Running-from-skunk guy

As far as the skunk goes, sometimes the officers propped open the door to the SHU recreation area to get fresh air. One evening, a skunk entered SHU. The officers tried to chase the animal out before it raised a stink, literally. They eventually coaxed the skunk out with a food trail of snack chips.

CHAPTER 26: Collateral Damage

My father was right. Working for the federal government was a good career. I never really worried about getting paid. There were a few occasions I thought the nonsense in Congress would cause a hitch. Fortunately, during my tenure, it did not. I could afford to retire at the age of fifty-five, two years before the mandatory retirement age. I had ten paid holidays, earned thirteen days of sick leave and twenty-six days of annual leave per year. I had excellent health benefits that I carried into retirement.

But with the benefits came a cost. Work in corrections changes a person, some more than others. These changes may range from subtle increases in suspiciousness to complete paranoia, from a little less empathy to cold-heartedness. Some staff carry a great deal of anger, some become alcoholics. I mentioned in an earlier chapter that I was aware I was growing more callous. I've also become more suspicious, more cynical, and more jaded. I hope, over time, some of this will dissipate.

I'm more vigilant when in public and have become a self-appointed pedophile profiler. While at waterparks, amusement parks, public parks, or

children's sporting events, I scan the crowd and try to identify pedophiles. When I'm in other public arenas, I don't necessarily search for it, but sometimes someone has the telltale signs and will catch my attention. I prefer to sit with my back to the wall when in restaurants.

I was also affected by the lack of quality support offered by the system. It's flawed, and not because of its treatment of inmates. It's flawed because of the treatment of staff. There's perpetual questioning and undermining of staff decisions — from those made by correctional officers to those made by wardens. A warden should be allowed to determine who, in their institution, needs to be in SHU and how to respond to accusations of sexual assault. If the organization doesn't have confidence in the warden's ability to do this, that person shouldn't be warden. A warden should have confidence in their correctional officers. If a correctional worker is unable to do the job, they shouldn't have the job. Trying to create broad policies for all institutions and situations, distrusting staff, requiring video evidence of misconduct is not a solution. There's something inherently wrong with a system that can't fire employees. There's something wrong with a system that's quick to believe the inmate over the officer. Attempts to correct the problems within the system doesn't seem to help at all. In fact, the solutions are

adding to the problem and are handicapping the officer. It's as if the solution is becoming the problem. The system needs to be revamped to create confidence in those in charge of the facility and rely less on the reports of those confined and those who are the ears and mouths of those confined.